CONTENTS

Introduction xi

History of Firehouse Cooking 1861-2021 xiii

BREAKFAST

Smoked Salmon, Scrambled Eggs and Spinach 1

Bratwurst Sausage and Red Onion Omelet 2

Fried Eggs and Bacon 3

Poached Eggs with Potato Pancakes 4

FDNY Engine 319 "The Lone Wolf" Individual Egg Muffins 5

American Breakfast Frittata 6

Blueberry Muffins 7

Banana Muffins 8

Pumpkin Spiced Muffins 9

Classic French Toast 10

Apple and Cinnamon Oatmeal 11

Fluffy American Pancakes 12

Crepes With Mixed Berries 13

Biscuits and Gravy 14

Buttermilk Biscuits 15

We Remember Quiche 16

MEAT

Jambalaya 19

007 Spaghetti and Meatballs 20

Brunswick Stew 21

Turkey Meatloaf 22

Chili Con Carne 23

Pork Tenderloin 24

FDNY Engine 305/Ladder 151 New York Strip Steak 25

Oven Baked BBQ Ribs 26

BBQ Beer Brats 27

Pulled Pork Burger 28

Pot Roast 29

Turkey Casserole 30

Beef Brisket 31

Huge Pork Chops 32

Beef Stew 33

Nicolosi Sausage & Lentil Stew 34

FISH

Shrimp and Grits 37

Lobster Rolls 38

Linguine with Clams 39

Maryland Crab Cakes 40

Mussels in Garlic Broth 41

Cajun Pecan Catfish 42

Clam Chowder 43

New Orleans Gumbo 44

FDNY Engine 299/Ladder 152 One Pan Baked Salmon and Vegetables ... 45

Seafood Pot Pie 46

Shrimp Bruschetta 47

CHICKEN

Reale Chicken Parmigiana 51

Chicken Pot Pie 52

Chicken Noodle Soup 53

Orange Chicken 54

Chicken and Dumplings 55

Chicken Fried Steak 56

Chicken Salad 57

Blackened Chicken 58

Chicken Casserinorole 59

AMERICAN FIREHOUSE CUISINE

Joseph T. Bonanno
City of New York Fire Department

Order this book online at www.trafford.com
or email orders@trafford.com

Most Trafford titles are also available at major online book retailers.

 www.trafford.com

North America & international
toll-free: 844 688 6899 (USA & Canada)
fax: 812 355 4082

Our mission is to efficiently provide the world's finest, most comprehensive book publishing service, enabling every author to experience success. To find out how to publish your book, your way, and have it available worldwide, visit us online at www.trafford.com

Because of the dynamic nature of the Internet, any web addresses or links contained in this book may have changed since publication and may no longer be valid. The views expressed in this work are solely those of the author and do not necessarily reflect the views of the publisher, and the publisher hereby disclaims any responsibility for them.

Any people depicted in stock imagery provided by Getty Images are models, and such images are being used for illustrative purposes only.
Certain stock imagery © Getty Images.

ISBN: 978-1-6987-0796-9 (sc)
ISBN: 978-1-6987-0797-6 (e)

Print information available on the last page.

Trafford rev. 07/21/2021

BBQ Chicken Wings 60

General Tso's Chicken 61

Kentucky Fried Chicken 62

RICE/POTATO/PASTA

Macaroni and Cheese 65

Penne alla Vodka 66

Chicken Alfredo 67

Baked Ziti 68

Chicken Riggies 69

Potato Salad 70

Stuffed Baked Potatoes 71

Cougzilla Mashed Potatoes 72

Vegetable Fried Rice 73

Pasta Il Pompiere 74

VEGETABLES

Waldorf Salad 77

Broccoli-Cauliflower Mash 78

Garlic Green Beans 79

Fried Green Tomatoes 80

Grilled Corn on The Cob 81

Collard Greens 82

Boston Beans 83

Three Bean Salad 84

Baked Artichoke Dip 85

THANKSGIVING

FDNY Engine 273/Ladder 129 Thanksgiving Stuffing 89

Roasted Turkey and Gravy 90

Can the Can Cranberry Sauce 91

DESSERT

Banana Bread Pudding..95

Firehouse Bread Pudding....................................96

Rice Pudding...97

Glazed Donut..98

Red Velvet Cake...99

Banana Foster..100

Texas Sheet Cake..101

POSA Cheesecake..102

Chocolate Sponge Cake.....................................103

Peach Cobbler..104

Chocolate Chip Cookies....................................105

Apple Pie...106

Blue Ribbon Carrot Cake...................................107

Normango Cobbler...108

Zucchini Bread..109

This book is dedicated to my father, Joseph T. Bonanno
from his son, Joseph T. Bonanno Jr.

I was a 21-year veteran of the FDNY (Engine 319, Ladder 129, Ladder 152) as well as my dear brother Michael FDNY (Engine 315, Engine 216, Ladder 7). We both proudly served the FDNY during the rescue and recovery at Ground Zero 9/11/01 and the weeks thereafter. Our choice to become firefighters was largely due to my father's pride and service being with the FDNY. He served in Engine 88 and Engine 306 through the 1960s and 1970s, the "war years" in the FDNY in the South Bronx.

Family issues caused separation from his children, sadly Michael Bonanno died by suicide in July of 2012. Family issues remained unsettled to his passing, which saddened us all but we, his children Joseph, Robert, Michael, and Donna, honor his service, to our country USN, the FDNY, his life and wish him peace and a gentle passing into God's loving hands. Every firefighter, especially FDNY earned this as did he.

Joseph T. Bonanno, Audrey
Bonanno and me!

Joseph T. Bonanno circa 1957
Engine 88 Bronx, NY

Joseph T. Bonanno, Joseph T. Bonanno Jr., Michael Bonanno
Graphite drawing by Joseph T. Bonanno Jr. with the excellent art instruction of Lee
Hammond. Signed prints available at www.americanfirehousecuisine.com

INTRODUCTION

September 11, 2021. Twenty years have passed since that God awful day. In my travels, one thing was universal. Everyone knew where they were and what they were doing on September 11, 2001. I have my own terrible story, as do so many but this is a cookbook, which will, as in my other books, celebrate one of the fondest "firehouse" traditions, the firehouse meals.

I was reminded of just how long it had been since my first two books, *The Healthy Firehouse Cookbook* and *The Firehouse Grilling Cookbook*. I was invited to do a cooking demonstration with the mayor of Plant City, Florida at their annual food bank party in 2012. After the event, the local firehouse came by to meet me. One of the firefighters on duty asked me to sign a book. Since he was a little child, his dream was to be a firefighter. His mother bought him anything firehouse related and bought my first cookbook for him on QVC. He then told me his mother bought it for him.... when he was 9 years old!!! He was 25 now and a firefighter with Plant City, Florida! Nice to know my book influenced him but also a wakeup call for me on how long it had been since my first cookbook!

So, I felt the timing was right for another cookbook. One because of how much time had passed and the other, the 20-year anniversary of 9/11. I have been blessed, first, working in the greatest job in the world, firefighting, in the greatest city to be one, New York City! I have been doubly blessed (and lucky) to be published as cookbook author. The books led to countless terrific experiences both in firehouses and media. I have met so many celebrities and cooked with Martha Stewart, Bobby Flay and Julia Child to name a few. I have cooked with and for firefighters in firehouses around the USA and been on many national and regional television shows. I have also been sort of a "celebrity chef" and appeared at culinary events.

After 9/11 and retiring, I also got my culinary degree to "professionalize" my cooking. Which is one of the reasons I called this book firehouse "Cuisine". In my travels, I had met and cooked with many firefighters whose "firehouse" cooking was on par with any professionals I had met. Firehouse cooking unfortunately had a reputation for being "meatloaf and mashed potatoes", grub type food. Sometimes yes, but when pressed, I and they can hold their own against the best and brightest culinary stars! Besides, some of those "basics" when done right, are superb! I have also experienced that giving a simple, basic recipe an outrageous name does not make it better. Such as a simple, well prepared gravy does not need to be renamed "gravy au jus with a turnip compote root reduction." It's gravy! Keep it simple, make it right and as we say in New York "I got your root reduction right here!" So, you will see many recipes contained within with simple names, done right, easy to make, easy to get ingredients for and tested not on TV or contest, tested with by world's toughest food critics, firefighters!

I cannot end the introduction without paying tribute to what we all lost 20 years ago on September 11, 2001. On that day, a day we will never forget, the lives of 343 firefighters were lost. In the subsequent 20 years many more lives including my brother, Michael of Ladder 7 FDNY were lost from cancers, disease, or suicide. Although I, too, was there on this day I am blessed to remain healthy. You can read more at my website www. americanfirehousecuisine.com. Portions of the proceeds from this book will be donated to www.ffbha.org, an organization that seeks to prevent firefighter suicides and assists families of victims.

History of Firehouse Cooking 1861-2021

As early as 1923, a Massachusetts fire chief was quoted in Firehouse Magazine praising firehouse cooking: "The experiments which have taken the form of newfangled ideas in cookery have met with such apparent success that there has been little or no sickness among firemen this year...such progress should be encouraged!" A few years earlier the same magazine sent two women to eat at a firehouse and reported that the meal was impressive and the dining room "rare and spotless."

Clearly, by the 1920s firehouse cooking was a firmly established practice that continues to this day. Firefighters began cooking for the on-duty crews early in the 1800s, when only volunteer fire departments existed in large cities. In those days, when the railroads were new, firefighters traveled between cities to visit other volunteer departments and compare notes on equipment, firefighting techniques, and operations. Whenever the out of towners arrived, along with accommodations, they were treated to a banquet at the firehouse.'

During the Civil War, New York Firefighters formed the first volunteer military outfit called the First Fire Zouaves. Eleven hundred strong, the Zouaves saw action at the Battle of Bull Run and other battlefields. In 1861, while stationed in Washington D.C., they assisted in putting out a fire next to the famous Willard Hotel and were honored at a banquet by the grateful hotel management. Sadly, the First Fire Zouaves were better trained to fight fires than battle Confederate soldiers and returned to New York with fewer than 300 men.

By the end of the Civil War, New York City established the nation›s first paid fire department, called the New York-Brooklyn Metropolitan Fire Department. Hiring preference was given to volunteers and by 1865 the department had six hundred paid firemen, thirty-three engines, eleven ladder apparatuses and was divided into companies of twelve men. The men worked constantly with three one-hour meal breaks per day and often went home to eat, had one day off per month for an annual salary of $700.

During those early days, the firehouse was mainly used to house the horses and equipment. By 1920, motorized fire apparatus replaced horses and the firehouses were remodeled. Haylofts became sleeping quarters and former horse stalls were dismantled to make way for kitchens and dining areas. The companies adopted a platoon system in which men alternated day and evening shifts and ate at least one meal at the firehouse. One man was appointed to cook and others to assist. It did not take long for firehouse food to gain a reputation as being hearty, plentiful and delicious.

Fast forward to 1984! John Sineno, NYC firefighter from Engine 58 in Harlem had gained a reputation as a good cook. He put together a small paperback book called *The Firefighters Cookbook* published in 1986. The Phil Donahue Show was moving from Chicago to New York and Phil Donahue asked how he could "warm up" to his new New York audience. The producers told him, do a "cooking segment." New Yorkers LOVE their firefighters and mentioned John Sinenos' book. The publishers did a small run of books, John thought it would only sell a few copies locally. John and several firefighters appeared on *The Phil Donahue Show* in 1986 and the timing was impeccable (even though John burnt the breaded chicken cutlet on air). The show, Phil Donahue and John Sineno were a huge hit. The book went on to be on the New York Times best seller list for 9 weeks! Firmly establishing "firehouse" cooking!

From then on, there were various firehouse cooking contests and tv appearances. I tried my hand at firehouse cooking, although after being certified as a fitness trainer and nutritionist, attempted to make some of the standard firehouse meals with an eye towards healthy. Yes, quite a few disasters and my sympathies to the members of Engine 273/Ladder 129 who were my test kitchen,

Fast forward again to 1993. The New School in Manhattan was offering a course for the first time "How to Write a Cookbook and Get It Published" I will admit I took the course more out of curiosity than anything else. The class was packed with potential cookbook authors, and I felt I was clearly out of my league...I was! In the afternoon, Harriet Bell, head editor of Broadway Books gave a dissertation on publishing a cookbook. She then opened the floor for ideas. Everyone's hand went up but mine. She shot down all the suggestions, even those with extensive culinary backgrounds! I was affirmed that I was out of my league!

I had mentioned my idea when the class started, mentioning John Sinenos' success and "if" I were to do a cookbook of firehouse recipes, it would be a "healthy" one. The teacher was closing the class and said don't be shy if you have a good idea...."like our fireman for instance". He asked me to mention the idea to the editor, I did, and she lit up, told me to see her after class. A longer story but I went on to publish *The Healthy Firehouse Cookbook*, the full story is in the introduction.

Continuing the story of Firehouse cooking, there was my first book in 1995 (thank you John Sineno!) *The Firehouse Grilling Cookbook* in 1998, Keith Young published *Cooking with The Firehouse Chef* in 2003 (who succumbed to cancer from working at the World Trade Center disaster) and there have been dozens of other "firehouse" cookbooks published in the USA and around the world. The media continues to embrace this tradition as firefighters, myself included, have appeared as guests and contestants on many regional and national television shows.

One day
you will be old,
you will be frail,
and you will be slow.

And someone will ask you,
"What did you do in your day?
What did you do in your prime?
When you were young and strong
and fast?"

You will tell them you were a New
York City Fireman,
and when the day is done
and the page is turned,
that will be enough.

BREAKFAST

Smoked Salmon, Scrambled Eggs and Spinach

SERVINGS: 1

TIME:
Preparation   5 minutes
Cooking   10 minutes
Total   15 minutes

EQUIPMENT:
Saucepan
Spatula

INGREDIENTS:
2 tbsp unsalted butter
3 eggs, lightly beaten
1 cup spinach
1 tbsp creme fraiche
2oz smoked salmon
2 slices sourdough bread, toasted
salt, to taste
black pepper, to taste

INSTRUCTIONS:
1. Place a saucepan on low heat, add 1 tbsp butter and eggs.
2. Stir the eggs with a spatula and scramble slowly for 5 minutes.
3. Once the eggs begin to thicken, add the spinach and fold through to wilt.
4. Remove the saucepan from the heat once the scrambled eggs are almost cooked, stir in 1 tbsp butter and creme fraiche.
5. Season the scrambled eggs and spinach with salt and black pepper to taste.
6. Plate a base of toasted sourdough, pour over scrambled eggs and spinach then top with the smoked salmon, serve hot.

BRATWURST SAUSAGE AND RED ONION OMELET

SERVINGS: 1

TIME:
Preparation   5 minutes
Cooking   10 minutes
Total   15 minutes

EQUIPMENT:
Sauté pan
Non-stick pan
Spatula

INGREDIENTS:
2 tbsp unsalted butter
3 oz bratwurst sausage, sliced at an angle
½ red onion, thinly sliced
½ cup mushroom, sliced
4 eggs, lightly beaten
salt, to taste

INSTRUCTIONS:
1. Place a sauté pan on medium heat and add 1 tbsp butter.
2. Then add the sliced red onion, cook to soften for 3 minutes.
3. Next add the bratwurst sausage and increase the heat of the pan to high. Sauté the sausages for 2 minutes to brown well.
4. Stir the mushrooms into the sausages and cook for a further 2 minutes.
5. Remove the sauté pan from the heat and set aside.
6. Place a non-stick pan on medium heat and add 1 tbsp butter.
7. Pour the egg into the pan and stir continuously with a spatula for 2 minutes.
8. The eggs will gradually begin to set while maintaining a smooth consistency. Remove the non-stick pan from the stove and add the cooked sausage, onion, mushroom, and salt.
9. Hold the pan at a downward angle onto a chopping board and tap the pan a few times to loosen the omelet.
10. Run a spatula round the sides of the omelet then gradually fold over onto the chopping board.
11. Transfer the bratwurst sausage and red onion omelet to a plate and serve immediately.

Fried Eggs and Bacon

SERVINGS: 1

TIME:
Preparation   5 minutes
Cooking   10 minutes
Total   15 minutes

EQUIPMENT:
Sauté pan

INGREDIENTS:
2 slices turkey bacon
1 tbsp vegetable oil
2 eggs
1 cup kale, roughly chopped
½ tsp chili flakes
salt, to taste
black pepper, to taste

INSTRUCTIONS:
1. Place a sauté pan on medium heat and add the turkey bacon.
2. Cook the bacon for 3 minutes then flip and cook for a further 3 minutes until crisp.
3. Transfer the bacon to a plate lined with kitchen paper and set aside.
4. Place the sauté pan back on the stove and add the vegetable oil.
5. Crack the two eggs into the pan and cook for 2 minutes until set with a runny yolk.
6. Remove the fried eggs onto the plate alongside the turkey bacon.
7. Stir the kale, garlic, and chili flakes into the sauté pan, cook for 2 minutes to soften and season with salt and black pepper.
8. Serve a bed of garlic and chili kale topped with the fried eggs and turkey bacon.

POACHED EGGS WITH POTATO PANCAKES

SERVINGS: 1

TIME:
Preparation   10 minutes
Cooking   20 minutes
Total   30 minutes

EQUIPMENT:
Colander
Saucepan
Slotted spoon
Sauté pan

INGREDIENTS:
Potato Pancake
6oz russet potato, peeled and grated
½ onion, grated
1 egg
1 tbsp all-purpose flour
¼ tsp onion powder
¼ tsp garlic powder
2 tbsp vegetable oil

Poached Eggs
2 eggs
2 tsp white wine vinegar
salt, to taste
black pepper, to taste

INSTRUCTIONS:
Potato Pancake
1. Place the grated potato and onion in a colander, season with 1 tsp salt and allow to sit for 2 mins. Then squeeze the excess moisture from the potato and onion, dry on a kitchen cloth.
2. In a mixing bowl add the egg, flour, onion powder, garlic powder, salt, and black pepper. Stir together to a smooth batter then add the potato and onion to the bowl, stir to combine.
3. Place a sauté pan on medium heat and add the vegetable oil.
4. Once the oil is shimmering, form the potato mixture into two pancakes and add to the sauté pan.
5. Cook the potato pancake for 5 minutes until golden brown then flip to cook the opposite side for 5 more minutes.
6. Remove the crispy potato cakes from the pan once cooked through and set aside to prepare the poached eggs.

Poached Eggs
1. Fill the saucepan halfway with water and bring the water to a boil, then add the white wine vinegar.
2. Reduce the saucepan to a simmer then crack the eggs directly into the pan. Crack the egg close to the water to ensure the poached egg stays intact.
3. Poach the eggs for 4 minutes until set, then remove onto a plate using a slotted spoon. Season the egg with salt and black pepper.
4. Lay two potato cakes on a plate and top each with a poached egg, serve. immediately.

FDNY ENGINE 319 "THE LONE WOLF" INDIVIDUAL EGG MUFFINS

Engine 319 was the first firehouse I was assigned to from the Probationary Fire Training Academy on Randalls Island. The "lone wolf" name in that it is a small, local firehouse, alone on a residential side street in Queens. It was there I was introduced to "family" style meals and firehouse cooking from some of the greats! Easy to cook for a small crew and where I first "experimented" cooking for firefighters! This recipe is a great way to get "on the go" nutrition, packed with protein.

SERVINGS: 12 muffins

TIME:
Preparation   15 minutes
Cooking   30 minutes
Total   45 minutes

EQUIPMENT:
Mixing bowl
Whisk
12 cup Muffin tray
Sauté pan

INGREDIENTS:
12 eggs, lightly beaten
1 tbsp vegetable oil
½ onion, finely chopped
1 clove garlic, finely chopped
8oz Italian sausage
½ cup cherry tomato, halved
1 cup cheddar cheese, grated
salt, to taste
black pepper, to taste

INSTRUCTIONS:
1.   Preheat an oven to 350 degrees Fahrenheit.
2.   In a mixing bowl whisk together the eggs, season with salt and black pepper.
3.   Place a sauté pan on medium heat and add the vegetable oil.
4.   Stir the chopped onion into the sauté pan and cook for 5 minutes to soften.
5.   Remove the sausage meat from the casings and add the sausage meat and garlic to the pan, use a spatula to break up the meat and brown all over.
6.   Once the sausage meat is cooked transfer the sausage and onion mixture into the muffin tray evenly between each cup.
7.   Fill the muffin cups with the cherry tomatoes and grated cheddar cheese.
8.   Then pour the egg mixture into each cup.
9.   Transfer the muffin tray to the preheated oven and bake for 20 minutes.
10. Remove the cooked individual egg muffins from the oven and allow to cool.
11. Serve two egg muffins per person, fillings can be varied with any cooked meat or vegetables which you prefer.

AMERICAN BREAKFAST FRITTATA

SERVINGS: 4

TIME:
Preparation   10 minutes
Cooking   30 minutes
Total   40 minutes

EQUIPMENT:
Non-stick oven-proof pan
Mixing bowl
Whisk

INGREDIENTS:
1 tbsp vegetable oil
6oz russet potato, peeled and diced
2oz bacon, diced
1 cup mushroom, sliced
6 eggs, lightly beaten
½ cup half and half
1 cup parmesan cheese, grated
salt, to taste
black pepper, to taste

INSTRUCTIONS:
1. Preheat an oven to 350 degrees Fahrenheit.
2. Place a non-stick pan on medium heat and add the vegetable oil.
3. Once hot, add the diced potato and season with salt and black pepper. Cook the potato for 3 minutes until golden brown.
4. Pour 2 tbsp water into the potatoes and cover with a lid to cook through for 3 minutes.
5. Transfer the cooked potato to a bowl and set aside.
6. Place the non-stick pan back on the heat and add the bacon, cook for 2 minutes until crisp.
7. Stir the mushroom into the pan with the bacon, cook for 2 minutes.
8. Reduce the heat to low, stir the cooked potatoes and parmesan cheese into the pan.
9. In a mixing whisk together the eggs and cream, pour into the pan and mix to combine.
10. Cook the frittata over a low heat on the stove for 5 minutes to begin to set the egg.
11. Transfer the frittata to the preheated oven for 15 minutes until set.
12. Allow the frittata to cool for 15 minutes then gently slide onto a chopping board.
13. Slice the American breakfast frittata and serve.

BLUEBERRY MUFFINS

SERVINGS: 12

TIME:
Preparation   15 minutes
Cooking   25 minutes
Total   40 minutes

EQUIPMENT:
Mixing bowl x 2
Whisk
Spatula
12 cup muffin tray
Muffin liners

INGREDIENTS:
2 cups all-purpose flour (plus 2 tbsp)
2 tsp baking powder
¼ tsp salt
1 cup caster sugar
2 eggs, lightly beaten
½ cup buttermilk
¼ cup vegetable oil
½ tsp vanilla extract
2 cups blueberries

INSTRUCTIONS:
1. Preheat an oven to 375 degrees Fahrenheit and line a muffin tray.
2. In a mixing bowl add the 2 cups flour, baking powder, salt, and caster sugar, whisk together to combine then set the dry ingredients aside.
3. Into a separate mixing bowl add the egg, buttermilk, vegetable oil and vanilla extract, whisk the wet ingredients until a uniform consistency.
4. Pour the bowl of wet ingredients into the bowl of dry ingredients, fold together to form a smooth batter.
5. Combine the blueberries with 2 tbsp flour, mix to coat the blueberries completely then add to the muffin batter.
6. Transfer the muffin batter evenly between the 12 muffin cups.
7. Place the muffin tray into the preheated oven and bake for 25 minutes.
8. Remove the blueberry muffins from the oven and allow to cool for 10 minutes.

BANANA MUFFINS

SERVINGS: 12

TIME:
Preparation   15 minutes
Cooking   20 minutes
Total   35 minutes

EQUIPMENT:
Mixing bowl x 2
Sieve
12 cup muffin tray
Muffin liners

INGREDIENTS:
3 bananas, ripe
2 eggs
¼ cup unsalted butter, melted
¼ cup sour cream
1 tsp vanilla extract
½ cup brown sugar
1 ½ cups all-purpose flour
1 tsp baking powder
1 tsp baking soda
½ tsp salt
½ tsp ground cinnamon

INSTRUCTIONS:
1. Preheat an oven to 375 degrees Fahrenheit.
2. Place a sieve over a mixing bowl and add the flour, baking powder, baking soda, salt, and ground cinnamon, set aside the dry ingredients.
3. In a second bowl add the ripe banana and mash with a fork until a puree.
4. Then add the egg, melted butter, sour cream, vanilla extract, and brown sugar into the mashed banana, stir to combine.
5. Pour the dry ingredients into the bowl of wet ingredients and fold together.
6. Line a muffin tray and scoop the batter evenly into each case.
7. Transfer the banana muffins into the preheated oven and bake for 5 minutes.
8. Reduce the oven temperature to 350 degrees Fahrenheit and bake for a further 15 minutes.
9. Remove the muffins from the oven and let them cool for 10 minutes.
10. Serve the baked banana muffins warm or at room temperature.

PUMPKIN SPICED MUFFINS

SERVINGS: 12 muffins

TIME:
Preparation   15 minutes
Cooking   22 minutes
Total   37 minutes

EQUIPMENT:
Sieve
Mixing bowl x 2
Whisk
Spatula
12 cup muffin tray
Muffin liners

INGREDIENTS:
1 ½ cups all-purpose flour
1 tsp baking soda
½ tsp baking powder
2 tsp ground cinnamon
¼ tsp ground nutmeg
½ tsp salt
½ cup vegetable oil
¼ cup milk
1 tsp vanilla extract
2 eggs, lightly beaten
½ cup caster sugar
½ cup brown sugar
1 cup pumpkin puree

INSTRUCTIONS:

1. Preheat an oven to 375 degrees Fahrenheit and line a muffin tray.
2. Place a sieve over a mixing bowl and add the flour, baking soda, baking powder, ground cinnamon and ground nutmeg. Sieve the dry ingredients into the mixing bowl then set aside.
3. In a second mixing bowl add the vegetable oil, milk, vanilla extract, eggs, caster sugar, brown sugar, and pumpkin puree, whisk the wet ingredients together until smooth.
4. Pour the dry ingredients into the bowl of wet ingredients, fold together with a spatula until just combined.
5. Divide the pumpkin batter evenly into the 12 muffin liners.
6. Place the muffin tray in the preheated oven and bake for 22 minutes.
7. Remove the baked pumpkin spiced muffins from the oven and allow to cool for 10 minutes before serving.

Classic French Toast

SERVINGS: 4 (2 slices of toast)

TIME:
Preparation   5 minutes
Cooking   25 minutes
Total   30 minutes

EQUIPMENT:
Mixing bowl
Whisk
Shallow dish
Sauté pan
Wire cooling rack

INGREDIENTS:
2 eggs
1 ½ cups milk
3 tbsp brown sugar
1 tsp vanilla extract
½ tsp ground cinnamon
¼ tsp ground nutmeg
¼ cup unsalted butter
8 thick slices bread, stale

INSTRUCTIONS:
1. Into a mixing bowl add eggs, milk, brown sugar, vanilla extract, ground cinnamon and ground nutmeg. Whisk together to form a smooth custard then pour the mixture into a shallow dish.
2. Place a slice of bread into the custard, allow to soak for 30 seconds then place on a tray and repeat for the remaining bread.
3. Place a sauté pan on medium heat and add 2 tbsp butter. Lay two slices of custard-soaked bread into the pan and cook for 3 minutes until golden brown.
4. Flip the toast and cook for a further 3 minutes.
5. Transfer the French toast to a cooling rack and continue to toast the bread in batches.
6. Serve the classic French toast warm with extra butter and melted syrup.

Apple and Cinnamon Oatmeal

SERVINGS: 4

TIME:
Preparation   5 minutes
Cooking   20 minutes
Total   25 minutes

EQUIPMENT:
Saucepan x 2

INGREDIENTS:
1 tsp unsalted butter
1 apple, roughly chopped
2 tsp brown sugar (optional)
½ tsp ground cinnamon
½ cup oats
½ cup water
1 cup milk (use soy or nut milk for vegan)
salt, to taste

INSTRUCTIONS:
1. Place a saucepan on medium heat and add the butter.
2. Then add the apples to the saucepan and cook for 5 mins, stirring occasionally.
3. Stir in the brown sugar and ground cinnamon to coat the apples, caramelize till brown and tender.
4. Remove the cinnamon apples for the stove and set aside.
5. Place a second saucepan on medium heat, add the oats, water, milk, and a pinch of salt.
6. Mix to combine the oats and liquid, bring to a simmer then reduce the heat to low.
7. Simmer the oatmeal for 20 minutes, stirring occasionally to prevent the oats from sticking to the bottom of the pan.
8. Adjust the oatmeal with extra water to achieve your desired consistency.
9. Serve the oatmeal warm topped with caramelized cinnamon apples.

FLUFFY AMERICAN PANCAKES

SERVINGS: 4 (8 pancakes)

TIME:
Preparation   5 minutes
Cooking   20 minutes
Total   25 minutes

EQUIPMENT:
Mixing bowl x 2
Sieve
Whisk
Non-stick pan
Spatula

INGREDIENTS:
1 ½ cups all-purpose flour
4 tsp baking powder
½ tsp fine salt
1 egg, lightly beaten
1 cup milk
¼ cup unsalted butter, melted (plus extra for cooking)
½ tsp vanilla extract

INSTRUCTIONS:
1. Into a mixing bowl sieve, the flour, baking powder and salt, set aside the dry ingredients.
2. In a second mixing bowl add the egg, milk, melted butter and vanilla extract, whisk together then pour the bowl of wet ingredients into the bowl of dry ingredients.
3. Stir the pancake batter together to form a smooth thick consistency.
4. Place a non-stick pan on medium heat and add 1 tsp butter.
5. Once the butter has melted add a ladle of pancake batter, cook for 2 minutes.
6. Flip the pancake and cook for a further 2 minutes until fluffy and golden brown.
7. Remove the cooked pancake from the pan and repeat the process with the remaining batter.
8. The pancakes are best served warm with maple syrup, honey, or fresh fruits.

CREPES WITH MIXED BERRIES

SERVINGS: 4

TIME:
Preparation   5 minutes
Cooking   15 minutes
Total   20 minutes

EQUIPMENT:
Mixing bowl
Whisk
Non-stick sauté pan
Ladle
Spatula

INGREDIENTS:
1 cup all-purpose flour
¾ cup milk
2 eggs, lightly beaten
3 tbsp unsalted butter, melted
1 tbsp caster sugar
1 tsp vanilla extract
¼ tsp salt
¼ cup unsalted butter, room temperature
1 cup Greek yogurt
1 cup blueberries
½ cup raspberries

INSTRUCTIONS:
1. Into a mixing bowl add the flour, milk, eggs, melted butter, sugar, vanilla extract and salt, whisk together the mixture to form a smooth uniform batter.
2. Cover the mixing bowl with plastic wrap and place in the refrigerator for 20 minutes, the batter can be made and then chilled the night before.
3. Once the batter has been chilled, place a sauté pan on medium heat and add 1 tsp butter.
4. Ladle ¼ cup of crepe batter into the preheated pan and lift the pan to spread the batter across the whole surface. Cook the crepe for 1 minute then use a spatula to swiftly flip the crepe onto the other side.
5. Cook the crepe for a further 1 minute until a light golden brown.
6. Transfer the cooked crepe to a plate and continue the process with the remaining batter.
7. Pour the Greek yogurt into a mixing bowl and whisk vigorously to thicken.
8. Fill the crepes with whipped yogurt and top with blueberries and raspberries.

BISCUITS AND GRAVY

SERVINGS: 4

TIME:
Preparation   15 minutes
Cooking   25 minutes
Total   40 minutes

EQUIPMENT:
Mixing bowl
Spatula
Rolling pin
Cast iron skillet
Baking tray
Parchment paper
Biscuit cutter

INGREDIENTS:
Biscuits
2 cup plain flour, plus extra for dusting
1 tbsp baking powder
½ tsp baking soda
½ tsp salt
1 ½ cup heavy cream

Gravy
1 tbsp unsalted butter
10 oz country sausage, removed from the casing
3 tbsp plain flour
2 cup milk
1 tsp Worcestershire sauce
salt, to taste
black pepper, to taste

INSTRUCTIONS:
Biscuits
1. Preheat an oven to 375 degrees Fahrenheit and line a baking tray with parchment paper.
2. In a mixing bowl combine the flour, baking powder, baking soda and salt.
3. Then pour the cream into the flour and bring together to form a thick dough.
4. Transfer the dough to a work surface and knead for 1 minute until smooth.
5. Dust a work surface with flour and roll the dough to ½-inch thick.
6. Cut the dough using a biscuit cutter and place the biscuits onto the baking tray.
7. Bake the biscuits in the preheated oven for 15 minutes until golden brown and doubled in size.

Gravy
1. Place a skillet on medium heat and add the butter.
2. Next add the sausage meat, cook the sausage for 8 minutes until well browned.
3. Stir the flour into the sausage and cook for 3 minutes.
4. Pour one cup of milk into the skillet and mix to a smooth texture.
5. Gradually add the remaining milk, stirring continuously to thicken.
6. Season the sausage gravy with Worcestershire sauce, salt, and black pepper to taste.
7. Serve the gravy over the warm biscuits.

BUTTERMILK BISCUITS

SERVINGS: 10

TIME:
Preparation   10 minutes
Cooking   12 minutes
Total   22 minutes

EQUIPMENT:
Baking tray
Mixing bowl
Saucepan
Wire cooling rack

INGREDIENTS:
3 cups all-purpose flour
1 tbsp sugar
1 tbsp baking powder
½ tsp baking soda
1 tsp salt
2 cups buttermilk

INSTRUCTIONS:
1. Preheat an oven to 450 degrees Fahrenheit and line a baking tray with parchment paper.
2. Into a mixing bowl add the flour, sugar, baking powder, baking soda and salt, stir to combine.
3. Place a saucepan on low heat and add the buttermilk, warm the buttermilk to a gentle simmer.
4. Pour the warm buttermilk into the mixing bowl of flour, stir to form a smooth dough.
5. Scoop two tablespoons of dough per biscuit onto the lined baking sheet, repeat to create 10 buttermilk biscuits.
6. Place the buttermilk biscuits into the preheated oven and bake for 12 minutes.
7. Remove the biscuits from the oven and cool on a wire rack.
8. Serve the buttermilk biscuits with softened butter.

WE REMEMBER QUICHE

SERVINGS: 8

TIME:
Preparation   30 minutes
Cooking   45 minutes
Total   1 hour 15 minutes

EQUIPMENT:
Pie tin
Mixing bowl x 2

INGREDIENTS:
9" pre-made pie crust
2 tsp hot brown mustard
4 slices Steak-umm, diced
¼ cup unsalted butter, diced
1 lb. asparagus, base trimmed and chopped
1 Vidalia onion,
2 cloves garlic, finely chopped
½ cup mushroom, sliced
4 eggs, lightly beaten
2 cups, skimmed mozzarella, shredded
¼ cup parsley, chopped
½ tsp salt
½ tsp black pepper
¼ tsp basil, thinly sliced
¼ tsp oregano, finely chopped
¼ tsp sage, finely chopped

Captain Jeff Dill
Palatine Rural Fire Protection
Inverness, IL
In 2011 Firefighter Behavioral Health Alliance was established by Jeff Dill to educate firefighters/EMS personnel and their families about behavioral health issues such as depression, PTSD, anxiety, and addictions as well as suicide, which is rampant in the fire service. He helped me immensely as I had lost my brother Michael, FDNY Ladder 7, to suicide in July of 2012. This delicious recipe was entered in the Steak-Umm Firefighter Cooking Contest. Please visit the website at www.ffbha.org and lend your support.

INSTRUCTIONS:
1. Preheat an oven to 375 degrees Fahrenheit.
2. Spread the hot brown mustard inside the pre-made pie crust to cover, set aside.
3. Place a skillet over medium heat and add the diced Steak-umm, brown for 1 minute then flip and cook for a further 30 seconds, remove the meat from the skillet and set aside.
4. Into the skillet add the butter and melt, then add the asparagus, onion, garlic, and mushrooms, cook for 5 minutes until the asparagus and onion are tender.
5. Transfer the cooked vegetables and Steak-umm to a mixing bowl and allow the ingredients to cool for 10 minutes.
6. In a separate mixing bowl whisk together the eggs, mozzarella, parsley, salt, black pepper, basil, oregano, and sage.
7. Stir the two mixing bowls together once the sauté mixture has cooled.
8. Pour the quiche mixture into the pie crust then place the quiche into the preheated oven for 30 minutes.
9. Remove the baked quiche from the oven and allow it to stand for 10 minutes before serving.

MEAT

JAMBALAYA

SERVINGS: 4

TIME:
Preparation   20 minutes
Cooking   30 minutes
Total   50 minutes

EQUIPMENT:
Saucepan with a lid

INGREDIENTS:
2 tbsp olive oil
1 red onion, finely chopped
1 red bell pepper, finely chopped
2 celery stalks, finely chopped
2 cloves garlic, finely chopped
10 oz andouille sausage, sliced
1 tbsp Creole seasoning
1 cup long grain rice
2 cup chicken broth
4 tomatoes, roughly chopped
10 oz raw shrimp
6 scallions, thinly sliced
1 tbsp parsley, finely chopped

INSTRUCTIONS:
1. Place a saucepan on medium heat and add the olive oil.
2. Then add the red onion, red pepper, and celery, cook for 5 minutes to soften.
3. Stir in the garlic, cook for 1 minute until fragrant.
4. Next add the andouille sausage, cook for 3 minutes to brown.
5. Then add the Creole seasoning and rice, stir through the saucepan to toast for 30 seconds.
6. Pour the chicken broth and tomato into the saucepan, stir to combine, and bring to a simmer.
7. Place a lid on the saucepan and reduce the heat to low, cook for 10 minutes.
8. Uncover the saucepan and add the shrimp, fold through the rice then cover the saucepan and cook for a further 5 minutes.
9. Garnish the jambalaya with sliced scallions and parsley, serve.

007 SPAGHETTI AND MEATBALLS

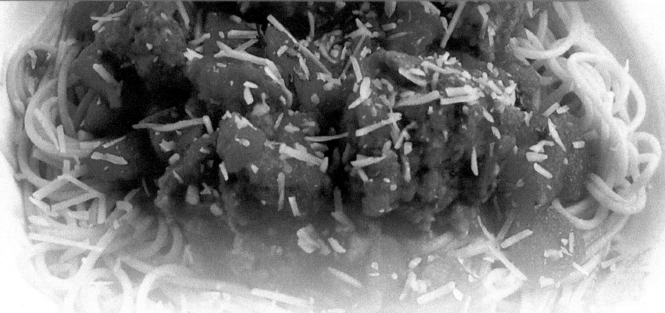

SERVINGS: 4

TIME:
Preparation   30 minutes
Cooking   40 minutes
Total   1 hour 10 minutes

EQUIPMENT:
Mixing bowl
Sauté pan
Saucepan x 2

INGREDIENTS:

Meatballs
½ cup breadcrumb
½ cup milk
½ cup parmesan cheese, grated
8 oz ground beef
8 oz ground pork
1 egg, lightly beaten
3 clove garlic, finely chopped
½ tsp rosemary, finely chopped
½ tsp black pepper
salt, to taste
1lb spaghetti

Marinara Sauce
2 tbsp olive oil
1 onion, finely chopped
2 clove garlic, finely chopped
2 tsp tomato paste
28 oz crushed tomatoes

Paul Thompson
Los Osos, CA
A dear friend to my firefighter brother Michael and me. In our "partying" days, Paul asked me once to prepare and entire dinner for a date he was having over his apartment. I did and brought it over, set it up on the stove and oven for him as if he had done it all himself. He proceeded to serve dinner and dessert for his date, who warmly replied, you did all this for me, it's delicious! I believe the night went well!

INSTRUCTIONS:

Meatballs
1. Into a mixing bowl add the breadcrumb and milk, allow the bread to soak for 2 minutes.
2. Then add the parmesan cheese, ground beef, ground pork, egg, garlic, rosemary, and black pepper. Combine the mixture then form, roll a golf-ball sized meatball in the palm of your hand then place on a tray, continue the process until all the mixture has been rolled into meatballs.
3. Place the tray of meatballs into the refrigerator for 20 minutes to firm up.

Marinara Sauce
1. While the meatballs are in the refrigerator, prepare the marinara sauce. Place a saucepan on medium heat and add one tablespoon of olive oil.
2. Then add the onion, cook for 5 minutes to soften.
3. Next add the garlic, cook for 1 minute until fragrant.
4. Stir in the tomato paste and cook out for 1 minute.
5. Pour the crushed tomatoes into the saucepan and bring to a simmer, cook for 20 minutes.
6. Place a sauté pan on medium heat and add one tablespoon of olive oil.
7. Then add the meatballs, cook for 5 minutes until browned well on all sides.
8. Transfer the meatballs to the saucepan of marinara sauce, allow to finish cooking in the sauce for 10 minutes.
9. Fill a saucepan with salted water and place on high heat. Bring the water to a boil and add the spaghetti.
10. Cook the spaghetti for 8 minutes then strain through a colander.
11. Stir the cooked pasta into the saucepan of meatballs, serve.

Brunswick Stew

SERVINGS: 4

TIME:
Preparation   20 minutes
Cooking   40 minutes
Total   1 hour

EQUIPMENT:
Saucepan

INGREDIENTS:
1 tbsp olive oil
2 onions, finely chopped
2 clove garlic, finely chopped
3 potatoes, peeled and diced
1 cup lima beans
2 cup chicken broth
1 tbsp Worcestershire sauce
1 cup barbeque sauce
28 oz crushed tomatoes
1 cup corn kernels
1 cup cooked chicken breast, shredded
1 cup cooked brisket, shredded (any leftover meat can be used such as sausages or pulled pork)
1 tsp black pepper
salt, to taste

INSTRUCTIONS:
1. Place a saucepan on medium heat and add the olive oil.
2. Then add the onion and garlic, cook for 5 minutes to soften.
3. Stir in the potato, lima beans, chicken broth, Worcestershire sauce, BBQ sauce and crushed tomatoes.
4. Bring the stew to a simmer and cook for 20 minutes until the potatoes and lima beans are tender.
5. Next add the corn, shredded chicken, brisket, season with black pepper and salt.
6. Warm the meat through the stew for 15 minutes then serve.

TURKEY MEATLOAF

SERVINGS: 6

TIME:
Preparation   20 minutes
Cooking   40 minutes
Total   1 hour

EQUIPMENT:
9"x13" Loaf tin
Mixing bowl
Sauté pan

INGREDIENTS:
1 tbsp vegetable oil
1 onion, finely chopped
2 cup mushroom, finely chopped
2 cloves garlic, finely chopped
1 tbsp Worcestershire sauce
¼ cup ketchup
1 cup breadcrumb
½ tsp thyme
½ tsp rosemary
2 eggs, lightly beaten
½ cup milk
1 lb. ground turkey
salt, to taste
black pepper, to taste

INSTRUCTIONS:
1. Preheat an oven to 400 degrees Fahrenheit and grease a loaf tin.
2. Place a sauté pan on medium heat and add the vegetable oil.
3. Then add the onion, cook for 5 minutes to soften.
4. Stir in the garlic and mushroom, cook for 8 minutes, and mix occasionally.
5. Then place the onion and mushroom mixture into a mixing bowl and allow to cool for 5 minutes.
6. Into the mixing bowl add the Worcestershire sauce, ketchup, breadcrumb, thyme, rosemary, egg, milk, ground turkey, season with salt and black pepper.
7. Bring the ingredients together lightly then transfer to the greased loaf tin.
8. Place the loaf tin in the preheated oven and bake for 45 minutes.
9. Once cooked, remove the meatloaf from the oven and allow it to stand for 10 minutes.
10. Turn the meatloaf out onto a chopping board and cut into thick slices, serve hot or cold.

CHILI CON CARNE

SERVINGS: 4

TIME:
Preparation   20 minutes
Cooking   1 hour
Total   1 hour 20 minutes

EQUIPMENT:
Saucepan

INGREDIENTS:
1 lb. ground beef
2 onions, finely chopped
3 clove garlic, finely chopped
1 tsp cayenne pepper
2 tsp ground coriander
2 tsp ground cumin
1 tbsp tomato paste
½ cup red wine
14 oz crushed tomatoes
1 cup beef broth
14 oz canned kidney beans, drained and rinsed
1 tsp smoked paprika
1 tsp oregano
salt, to taste
black pepper, to taste

INSTRUCTIONS:
1. Place a saucepan on high heat and add the ground beef, cook for 5 minutes until well browned.
2. Transfer the browned beef to a plate and set aside, into the saucepan add the onion.
3. Cook the onion for 5 minutes to soften.
4. Then add the garlic, cayenne, coriander, and cumin, cook for 1 minute until fragrant.
5. Stir in the tomato paste and cook for a further 1 minute.
6. Pour the red wine into the saucepan and reduce the liquid by half.
7. Next return the browned beef to the pan along with the crushed tomato and beef broth.
8. Bring the chili con carne to a simmer and cook gently for 45 minutes.
9. Once the sauce has thickened and the beef is tender, add the kidney beans, paprika, oregano, salt, and black pepper.
10. Bring the flavors together in the saucepan for 5 minutes then serve the chili con carne over boiled rice.

PORK TENDERLOIN

SERVINGS: 6

TIME:
Preparation   20 minutes
Cooking   1 hour
Total   1 hour 20 minutes

EQUIPMENT:
Zester
Kitchen twine
Sauté pan
Wire rack
Baking tray

INGREDIENTS:
3 lb. pork tenderloin, trimmed
1 lemon, zested
4 cloves garlic, finely chopped
½ cup parsley, finely chopped
2 tbsp rosemary, finely chopped
¼ cup olive oil
salt, to taste

INSTRUCTIONS:
1. Remove the pork tenderloin from the refrigerator and allow it to come to room temperature for 30 minutes.
2. In a bowl combine the lemon zest, garlic, parsley, rosemary, and olive oil, stir to form a thick herb paste.
3. Preheat an oven to 325F and roast for 1 hour.
4. Using a long sharp knife slice into the pork along the length of the tenderloin, opening the meat into one long piece.
5. Lay the pork fat-side down and season with salt, then spread the herb paste across the inside of the meat.
6. Then roll the pork back up and secure by tying kitchen twine every inch across the length of the meat.
7. Place the pork onto an oven rack set over a baking tray and roast for 45 minutes.
8. After 45 minutes place a sauté pan on high heat and add the pork tenderloin, sear for 2 minutes per side to develop a deep brown crust.
9. Allow the tenderloin to rest for 5 minutes then carve into thick slices and serve.

FDNY Engine 305/Ladder 151 New York Strip Steak

SERVINGS: 4

TIME:
Preparation   5 minutes
Cooking   20 minutes
Total   25 minutes

EQUIPMENT:
Cast-iron skillet

INGREDIENTS:
2 tbsp olive oil
4 New York Strip Steak (8-10 oz)
4 clove garlic, peeled
4 sprig thyme
4 sprig rosemary
¼ cup unsalted butter
salt, to taste
black pepper, to taste

Probably my best 6 months on the FDNY! After working in Engine 319, small, single Engine firehouse with a crew of 4 and after a family tragedy, my captain suggested a tour of duty in a "truck" company. So, I was UFO (Until Further Orders) assigned to Ladder 151 on Queens Blvd. When the firehouse was built, the residents wanted it to blend in with local architecture, so it is one of the most beautiful buildings in the area. Crew of 12, big, well prepared meals and a crew of characters like no other. The laughs alone were worth it!

INSTRUCTIONS:
1. Remove the steaks from the refrigerator and allow to come to room temperature for 20 minutes, pat the surface of the meat dry with a kitchen towel.
2. Season the NY Strip Steak with salt and pepper, set aside for 10 minutes.
3. Place a skillet on high heat and add the olive oil.
4. Once hot, lay the steak into the pan and add the garlic, thyme, and rosemary.
5. Sear the steak for 3 minutes then flip and cook for a further 3 minutes.
6. Next add the butter to the pan, tilt the pan towards you and use a spoon to baste the steak with the foaming butter.
7. Transfer the steak to a plate and pour the garlic herb butter over the surface.
8. Allow the New York Strip Steak to rest for 5 minutes then serve with the pan juices.

Oven Baked BBQ Ribs

SERVINGS: 4

TIME:
Preparation   15 minutes
Cooking   2 hours 30 minutes
Total   2 hours 45 minutes

EQUIPMENT:
Mixing bowl
Baking tray
Aluminum foil
Saucepan

INGREDIENTS:

Oven Baked Ribs
¼ cup brown sugar
2 tsp cayenne pepper
2 tsp smoked paprika
1 tsp mustard powder
1 tsp garlic powder
1 tsp onion powder
1 tsp salt
½ tsp black pepper
1 rack baby back ribs, membrane removed

BBQ SAUCE
½ cup ketchup
½ cup water
¼ cup brown sugar
¼ cup apple cider vinegar
1 tbsp molasses
2 tsp Worcestershire sauce

INSTRUCTIONS:
1. Preheat an oven to 300 degrees Fahrenheit and line a baking tray with aluminum foil.
2. In a mixing bowl combine the brown sugar, cayenne, paprika, mustard powder, garlic powder, onion powder, salt, and black pepper, stir to form the spice rub.
3. Slice the rack into individual ribs then add to the mixing bowl of spice rub, toss the ribs to coat with the rub.
4. Transfer the ribs to the baking tray and spread into an even layer, cover the tray with aluminum foil and bake for 2 hours 30 minutes.
5. While the ribs bake prepare the BBQ sauce, into a saucepan add the ketchup, water, brown sugar, apple cider vinegar, molasses, and Worcestershire sauce.
6. Place the saucepan of BBQ sauce on a medium heat and bring to a boil.
7. Then reduce to a simmer and cook for 15 minutes, stirring occasionally. Once the sauce is thick enough to coat the back of a spoon remove from the heat and set aside.
8. Then remove the ribs from the oven and discard the aluminum foil cover.
9. Set the oven to broil and coat the ribs in BBQ sauce.
10. Cook the oven baked BBQ ribs for 5 minutes until sticky and glazed.
11. Allow the ribs to rest for 5 minutes then serve.

BBQ BEER BRATS

SERVINGS: 4

TIME:
Preparation   10 minutes
Cooking   30 minutes
Total   40 minutes

EQUIPMENT:
Saucepan
BBQ / Griddle pan

INGREDIENTS:
1 tbsp unsalted butter
1 onion, thinly sliced
1 green bell pepper, thinly sliced
1 clove garlic, finely chopped
24 oz dark beer
2 tbsp brown sugar
¼ cup apple cider vinegar
8 bratwurst sausages (approximately 2lb)
black pepper, to taste
8 buns, halved
2 tbsp dark mustard

INSTRUCTIONS:
1. Place a saucepan on medium heat and add the butter.
2. Then add the onion and bell pepper, cook for 5 minutes to soften.
3. Stir in the garlic and cook for 1 minute.
4. Pour the dark beer, brown sugar, apple cider vinegar and black pepper into the saucepan, mix to combine.
5. Next add the bratwurst sausages and bring the saucepan to a gentle simmer, cook for 15 minutes.
6. Preheat a BBQ or griddle pan and remove the brats from the saucepan.
7. Grill the brats for 10 minutes until crisp and browned all over.
8. Serve the BBQ beer brats in a bun with mustard and top with the beer-braised onion and bell pepper.

PULLED PORK BURGER

SERVINGS: 6

TIME:
Preparation 20 minutes
Cooking 4 hours 30 minutes
Total 4 hours 50 minutes

EQUIPMENT:
Roasting tray
Aluminum foil
Saucepan
Mixing bowl

INGREDIENTS:

Spice Rub
4 tbsp brown sugar
1 tbsp smoked paprika
2 tsp onion powder
2 tsp garlic powder
1 tsp mustard powder
1 tsp ground cinnamon
½ tsp black pepper
salt, to taste
2 lb. pork shoulder, trimmed
1 cup cider

BBQ Sauce
1 cup ketchup
1 cup brown sugar
¼ cup apple cider vinegar
3 tbsp soy sauce
3 tbsp unsalted butter
½ cup water
6 burger buns, halved

INSTRUCTIONS:

1. Preheat an oven to 400 degrees Fahrenheit and line a roasting tray with aluminum foil.
2. Into a mixing bowl add the brown sugar, paprika, onion powder, garlic powder, mustard powder, ground cinnamon, black pepper, and salt to form the spice rub.
3. Apply the spice rub to the pork shoulder to coat all the surfaces then place in the roasting tray.
4. Roast the pork shoulder for 30 minutes.
5. Remove the pork shoulder from the oven and add the cider, cover the tray with aluminum foil and reduce the oven temperature to 300 degrees Fahrenheit.
6. Slow cook the pork shoulder covered for 4 hours.
7. While the pork cooks prepare the BBQ sauce, in a saucepan add one tablespoon spice rub, ketchup, brown sugar, apple cider vinegar, soy sauce, butter and water.
8. Place the saucepan on low heat and bring to a simmer, cook for 20 minutes.
9. Once cooked, remove the pork from the oven and shred with two forks.
10. Pour the BBQ sauce into the pulled pork.
11. Serve the pulled pork within the burger buns topped with extra BBQ sauce.

POT ROAST

SERVINGS: 6

TIME:
Preparation   20 minutes
Cooking   3 hours 15 minutes
Total   3 hours 35 minutes

EQUIPMENT:
Dutch oven

INGREDIENTS:
3lb beef roast, boneless
3 tsp salt
2 tsp black pepper
2 tbsp plain flour
1 tbsp vegetable oil
1 cup red wine
4 clove garlic, finely chopped
1 bay leaf
3 sprig thyme
1 tbsp Dijon mustard
2 onions, roughly chopped
2 celery stalks, roughly chopped
4 carrots, roughly chopped
3 cup potato, roughly chopped

INSTRUCTIONS:
1. Pat the beef roast dry with kitchen paper and season with salt and black pepper. Allow the meat to come to room temperature for 30 minutes and preheat an oven to 300 degrees Fahrenheit.
2. Place a wide Dutch oven on medium heat and add the vegetable oil.
3. Dust the beef roast with flour to cover then lay into the Dutch oven, sear for 5 minutes without moving to achieve a deep caramelized crust.
4. Then flip the beef roast and cook for a further 5 minutes on the other side.
5. Remove the beef roast from the pan and set aside.
6. Deglaze the pot with the red wine and bring to a simmer.
7. Then add the garlic, bay leaf, thyme, Dijon mustard, onion, and celery.
8. Return the beef roast to the Dutch oven and cover with a lid.
9. Transfer the pot roast to the oven for 2 hours.
10. After 2 hours remove the pot roast from the oven, add the carrot and potato to the pot. Roast for a further 1 hour in the oven.
11. Serve the pot roast hot alongside the braised carrot and potatoes then top with sauce.

TURKEY CASSEROLE

SERVINGS: 8

TIME:
Preparation   15 minutes
Cooking   35 minutes
Total   50 minutes

EQUIPMENT:
Saucepan
Casserole dish

INGREDIENTS:
3 tbsp unsalted butter
1 onion, roughly chopped
1 red bell pepper, roughly chopped
2 cup mushroom, roughly chopped
3 tbsp plain flour
½ cup white wine
2 tsp thyme
1 tsp tarragon
2 tsp Dijon mustard
2 cup chicken broth
¼ cup cream
1 cup pepper jack cheese, grated
2 cup cooked turkey, shredded
1 cup peas
¼ cup parsley, finely chopped
½ cup breadcrumb

INSTRUCTIONS:
1. Preheat an oven to 375 degrees Fahrenheit.
2. Place a saucepan on medium heat and add butter.
3. Then add the onion, red pepper, and mushroom, cook for 5 minutes to soften.
4. Stir the flour into the pan, stir constantly to cook out the flour for 2 minutes.
5. Pour the white wine into the pan and stir to bring together.
6. Next add the thyme, tarragon Dijon and chicken broth, stir into a thick smooth sauce.
7. Bring the sauce to a simmer and add cream, cheese, turkey, peas, and parsley, mix to combine.
8. Transfer the mixture to a casserole dish and spread to an even layer.
9. Top the casserole with breadcrumbs and place in the preheated oven.
10. Bake the casserole for 20 minutes until bubbling with a golden breadcrumb crust.

Beef Brisket

SERVINGS: 8

TIME:
Preparation   15 minutes
Cooking   5 hour 30 minutes
Total   30 minutes

EQUIPMENT:
Cast iron skillet
Aluminum foil

INGREDIENTS:
4 lb. beef brisket
2 tsp mustard powder
2 tsp ground cumin
2 tsp cayenne pepper
1 tsp black pepper
1 tsp salt
1 tbsp vegetable oil
2 onions, sliced
1 tbsp brown sugar
1 tsp tomato paste
12 oz beer
2 cup beef broth

INSTRUCTIONS:
1. Preheat an oven to 300 degrees Fahrenheit.
2. Into a bowl combine the mustard powder, ground cumin, cayenne pepper, black pepper, and salt to create a spice rub.
3. Apply the spice mix to cover the brisket and rub into the meat.
4. Place a cast iron skillet on high heat and add vegetable oil.
5. Lay the spiced beef brisket into the skillet and sear for 3 minutes then flip and cook for a further 3 minutes.
6. Remove the brisket from the skillet and set aside.
7. Reduce the heat of the skillet to medium, stir in the onion and brown sugar, cook for 3 minutes.
8. Then add the tomato paste and cook for 1 minute.
9. Pour the beer and beef broth into the skillet and bring to a simmer.
10. Return the seared brisket to the skillet then cover with aluminum foil.
11. Place the beef brisket in the oven and braise for 4 hours until tender.
12. Allow the beef to rest for 10 minutes then serve topped with cooking juices.

HUGE PORK CHOPS

Officer Scott Lasco
New York City Police Department
Highway Division

SERVINGS: 4

TIME:
Preparation   15 minutes
Marinate   2 hour - Overnight
Cooking   15 minutes
Total   2 hour 30 minutes

EQUIPMENT:
Mixing bowl
Whisk
Sauté pan

INGREDIENTS:
1 cup pineapple juice
¼ cup brown sugar
¼ cup ketchup
¼ cup soy sauce
2 clove garlic, finely chopped
1 tsp ground ginger
2 tbsp lime juice
4 pork chops (approximately 2lb)
1 tbsp vegetable oil

INSTRUCTIONS:
1. In a bowl whisk together the pineapple juice, brown sugar, ketchup, soy sauce, garlic, ginger, and lime juice to form the sauce
2. Transfer half of the sauce to a Ziplock bag and add the pork chops, ensure the pork is covered in sauce then refrigerate for at least 2 hours.
3. Once marinated, remove the pork chops from the marinade and pat dry with kitchen paper.
4. Place a sauté pan on high heat and add the vegetable oil.
5. Lay the marinated pork chops into the pan and sear for 2 minutes then flip and cook for a further 2 minutes.
6. Pour the remaining sauce into the sauté pan and bring to a simmer, cook the chops in the sauce for 5 minutes basting occasionally.
7. Serve the pork chops covered in the sweet thick sauce.

BEEF STEW

SERVINGS: 6

TIME:
Preparation   20 minutes
Cooking   2 hour
Total   30 minutes

EQUIPMENT:
Dutch oven

INGREDIENTS:
½ cup plain flour, plus 1 tbsp
2 tsp salt
1 tsp black pepper
2lb beef chuck roast, diced to 2-inch cubes
2 tbsp vegetable oil
1 onion, finely chopped
1 cup mushroom, sliced
2 clove garlic, finely chopped
2 tbsp tomato paste
1 cup red wine
4 cup beef broth
1 bay leaf
1 sprig rosemary
3 carrots, roughly chopped
2 celery stalks, roughly chopped
2 cup potato, roughly chopped
¼ cup parsley, finely chopped

INSTRUCTIONS:
1. Into a mixing bowl combine the ¼ cup flour, salt, and black pepper.
2. Then add the diced beef to the flour and toss to coat, shake off any excess flour.
3. Place a Dutch oven on medium heat and add the vegetable oil.
4. Cook the beef in batches for 5 minutes until well browned then remove the beef from the pan and set aside.
5. Then add the onion and mushroom, cook for 5 minutes.
6. Stir in the garlic, cook for 1 minute.
7. Next add the tomato paste and flour, cook for 2 minutes until thick.
8. Pour the wine into the Dutch oven to deglaze, stir to combine into a thick sauce with the flour.
9. Then add the beef broth, bay leaf, rosemary, and seared beef.
10. Bring the stew to a boil then reduce the heat to a simmer, cook for 1 hour.
11. After 1 hour, add the carrot, celery, and potato. Cover the stew and cook for 30 minutes.
12. Once the beef is tender with a thick and rich sauce, serve garnished with fresh parsley.

Nicolosi Sausage & Lentil Stew

Michael Nicolosi, Donna Nicolosi
Nicholas, Jake, and Jessica Nicolosi
Mike served as a police officer with the NYPD and then the Suffolk County Police Department attaining the rank of Sergeant. This is our "go to" recipe for a great one pot meal at home or firehouse. Delicious, easy to make and hits all the marks for good nutrition. P. S. My brother in law, sister, niece and nephews!

SERVINGS: 8

TIME:
Preparation   15 minutes
Cooking   1 hour
Total   1 hour 15 minutes

EQUIPMENT:
Large saucepan

INGREDIENTS:
1 tbsp olive oil
8 oz hot Italian turkey sausage, pierced with a fork
8 oz sweet Italian turkey sausage, pierced with a fork
1 onion, finely chopped
2 clove garlic, minced
6 cups chicken broth
1 ½ cups water
1 lb. dried lentils, rinsed with cold water
28 oz canned stewed tomatoes
½ tsp dried oregano
½ tsp dried tarragon
½ tsp black pepper
½ tsp sugar
¼ tsp hot red pepper sauce

INSTRUCTIONS:
1. Place a large saucepan on medium heat and add the olive oil.
2. Then add the turkey sausages to the pan and cook for 8 minutes, turn occasionally to brown on all sides.
3. Transfer the cooked sausages to a plate and cut into ¼-inch thick slices.
4. Reserve one tablespoon of pork fat for cooking, then add the onion and garlic, cook for 3 minutes to soften.
5. Into the saucepan add the sliced sausages, chicken broth, water, and lentils.
6. Bring the stew to a boil then reduce the heat to a simmer, cook for 30 minutes.
7. Stir in the stewed tomatoes, oregano, tarragon, black pepper, sugar, and hot pepper sauce, cook for a further 20 minutes until the lentils are tender.

FISH

SHRIMP AND GRITS

SERVINGS: 4

TIME:
Preparation   10 minutes
Cooking   35 minutes
Total   45 minutes

EQUIPMENT:
Saucepan with a lid
Sauté pan
Mixing bowl

INGREDIENTS:

Grits
1 cup chicken broth
1 cup milk
½ cup quick grits
½ cup cheddar cheese, grated
2 tbsp unsalted butter
1 tsp garlic powder
½ tsp paprika
salt, to taste
black pepper, to taste

Shrimp
12 oz jumbo shrimp, peeled and deveined
2 tsp Cajun seasoning
5 oz bacon, chopped
2 tbsp unsalted butter
½ cup onion, finely chopped
½ cup green bell pepper, finely chopped
2 clove garlic, finely chopped
1 tbsp all-purpose flour
½ cup chicken broth
½ lemon, juiced
4 scallions, thinly sliced

INSTRUCTIONS:

Grits
1. Place a saucepan on high heat, add the chicken broth and milk.
2. Bring the liquid to a boil then gradually pour the quick grits into the saucepan, stirring continuously.
3. Reduce the heat to medium-low and continue to stir for 5 minutes until thickened.
4. Then stir in the cheddar cheese, butter, garlic powder, paprika, salt, and black pepper.
5. Cover the saucepan with a lid and allow the grits to cook for 5 minutes.
6. Once the grits are smooth and creamy, remove the saucepan from the heat and cover with a lid to keep warm.

Shrimp
1. In a mixing bowl combine the shrimp and Cajun seasoning, stir to coat the shrimp.
2. Place a sauté pan on medium heat and add the chopped bacon.
3. Cook the bacon for 5 minutes until crispy and the fat has rendered.
4. Transfer the cooked bacon to a plate lined with kitchen paper.
5. Then add the shrimp to the sauté pan with bacon fat, cook for 1 minute per side.
6. Once cooked, remove the shrimp from the pan and place onto the plate with the bacon.
7. Next add the butter to the sauté pan and allow it to melt.
8. Stir the onion and green bell pepper into the pan, cook for 5 minutes to soften.
9. Then add the chopped garlic and flour, stir for 1 minute.
10. Pour the chicken broth into the pan, mix to form a thick and smooth sauce.
11. Return the shrimp and bacon to the sauté pan to reheat.
12. Season the shrimp with fresh lemon juice, salt, and black pepper.
13. Serve a generous spoonful of grits then top with the shrimp, garnish the plate with scallions and serve.

LOBSTER ROLLS

SERVINGS: 4

TIME:
Preparation   25 minutes
Cooking   20 minutes
Total   45 minutes

EQUIPMENT:
Saucepan
Mixing bowl
Sauté pan

INGREDIENTS:
1 ½ lb. lobster, live
¼ cup unsalted butter
4 bread rolls, cut open along the top
¼ tsp oregano
¼ tsp thyme
¼ tsp black pepper
1 lemon, quartered
¼ cup chives, finely chopped

INSTRUCTIONS:
1. Place a large saucepan of water on high heat and bring to a boil.
2. Season the water generously with salt.
3. Set the lobster on a chopping board and position a knife at the center of the lobster's head.
4. Slice down in one swift fast motion to cut through the lobster's head.
5. Place the lobster into the saucepan of boiling water and reduce the heat to a simmer.
6. Cook the lobster for 6 minutes and prepare a mixing bowl filled with iced water.
7. Transfer the cooked lobster to the bowl of iced water and chill.
8. Once chilled, remove the lobster from the iced water and place onto a chopping board.
9. Remove the claws from the lobster and twist the pincer to remove, crack the claw with the back of a knife and remove the lobster meat.
10. Detach each leg and snap at the joint, use tweezers or the back of a teaspoon to remove the leg meat.
11. Then place the tail on a chopping board and through the middle, remove the dark vein from the lobster and discard.
12. Chop the lobster meat into bite-sized pieces and place into a bowl.
13. Place a sauté pan on medium heat and add one tablespoon of butter.
14. Then add the bread rolls into the butter, cook on each side for 2 minutes until toasted.
15. Remove the toasted rolls from the pan and set aside.
16. Next add the remaining butter to the sauté pan along with the lobster meat, oregano, thyme, and black pepper, warm through for 2 minutes.
17. Take the sauté pan off the heat and begin to build the lobster rolls.
18. Fill the toasted rolls with the buttery lobster mixture then top with chopped chives and a squeeze of lemon juice.

Linguine with Clams

SERVINGS: 4

TIME:
Preparation   10 minutes
Cooking   12 minutes
Total   22 minutes

EQUIPMENT:
Large sauté pan
Saucepan

INGREDIENTS:
1 cup olive oil
6 clove garlic, thinly sliced
1 tsp chili flakes
1 lb. fresh clams
1 cup white wine
1 cup parsley, finely chopped
12 oz linguine
1 lemon, juiced
salt, to taste
black pepper, to taste

INSTRUCTIONS:
1. Place a saucepan of water on high heat and bring to a boil.
2. Season the boiling water with salt then add the linguine.
3. Cook the linguine for 6 minutes.
4. While the linguine cooks, place a sauté pan on medium heat and add the olive oil.
5. Stir the garlic and chili flakes into the sauté pan, cook for 1 minute.
6. Pour the white wine into the sauté pan and bring to a boil.
7. Then add the whole clams and parsley to the pan.
8. Cook for 3 minutes until the clams begin to open.
9. Transfer the linguine to the sauté pan and mix through the clams, add ½ cup of the pasta cooking water.
10. Cook the linguine in the clam sauce for 2 minutes until tender, season with lemon juice, salt, and black pepper.
11. Serve the linguine with clams immediately.

MARYLAND CRAB CAKES

SERVINGS: 4

TIME:
Preparation   20 minutes
Cooking   10 minutes
Total   30 minutes

EQUIPMENT:
Mixing bowl
Sauté pan

INGREDIENTS:
½ cup mayonnaise
1 egg, lightly beaten
1 tbsp Dijon mustard
1 tbsp Worcestershire sauce
1 tbsp Old Bay seasoning
2 tbsp parsley, finely chopped
½ cup crackers, finely ground
1 ½ lb. lump crab meat
2 tbsp unsalted butter

INSTRUCTIONS:
1. Into a mixing bowl add mayonnaise, egg, Dijon mustard, Worcestershire sauce, old bay seasoning, parsley, and crackers.
2. Stir the ingredients to combine evenly into a thick paste.
3. Then add the crab meat and gently fold through the ingredients in the mixing bowl.
4. Divide the crab mixture into four and use your hands to form into compact crab cakes.
5. Place a sauté pan on medium heat and add the butter.
6. Lay the crab cakes into the sauté pan, cook for 2 minutes until crisp and golden brown.
7. Flip the crab cakes and cook for a further 2 minutes.
8. Serve the Maryland crab cakes warm alongside a light salad or tartare sauce.

MUSSELS IN GARLIC BROTH

SERVINGS: 4

TIME:
Preparation   10 minutes
Cooking   10 minutes
Total   20 minutes

EQUIPMENT:
Large saucepan with a lid

INGREDIENTS:
2 tbsp unsalted butter
1 onion, finely chopped
4 clove garlic, finely chopped
½ tsp chili flakes
1 lemon, zested and quartered
2 cup white wine
4 lb. mussels, scrubbed and debearded
½ cup parsley, roughly chopped
crusty bread, to serve

INSTRUCTIONS:
1. Place a large saucepan on medium heat and add the butter.
1. Stir in the onion and cook for 5 minutes to soften.
2. Then add the garlic and chili flakes, cook for 1 minute until fragrant.
3. Pour the lemon zest and white wine into the saucepan.
4. Increase the heat of the stove to high and bring the wine to a boil.
5. Then add the mussels to the saucepan and cover with a lid.
6. Cook the mussels for 2 minutes, occasionally shake the pan to encourage the mussels to open.
7. Stir the chopped parsley into the saucepan and cook for a further minute until all the mussels have opened (if any mussels have not opened by this stage, then discard).
8. Transfer the mussels to four bowls and spoon over the garlic broth.
9. Serve with crusty bread and a squeeze of fresh lemon juice.

Cajun Pecan Catfish

SERVINGS: 4

TIME:
Preparation   20 minutes
Cooking   10 minutes
Total   30 minutes

EQUIPMENT:
Mixing bowl x 3
Food processor
Sauté pan

INGREDIENTS:
1 ½ lb. catfish fillets, cut into 4 oz pieces
2 tsp smoked paprika
1 tsp salt
½ tsp black pepper
2 tsp Cajun seasoning
1 cup pecans, roasted
½ cup cornmeal
½ cup all-purpose flour
2 eggs, lightly beaten
¼ cup vegetable oil

INSTRUCTIONS:
1. Into a mixing bowl add the catfish fillets, smoked paprika, salt, black pepper and one teaspoon of Cajun seasoning. Toss to coat the fish in the spices and set aside.
2. In a food processor add the roasted pecans, cornmeal and remaining Cajun seasoning, blitz to a fine crumb.
3. Set up three bowls, in one add the flour, then into the second add the beaten egg and into the third add the Cajun pecan crumb.
4. Take a fillet of catfish and place into the bowl of flour to coat, dust off any excess flour.
5. Then dip the floured catfish into the egg and finally dip into the Cajun pecan crumb, press the catfish fillet to coat completely.
6. Place the Cajun pecan catfish on a plate and repeat the breading process for the remaining fillets.
7. Set a sauté pan on medium heat and add the vegetable oil.
8. Lay the catfish into the sauté pan, cook for 3 minutes then flip and cook for a further 3 minutes.
9. Remove the catfish from the sauté pan once golden brown and crisp.
10. Serve the Cajun pecan catfish hot with rice, salad, or sweet potato.

Clam Chowder

SERVINGS: 4

TIME:
Preparation   20 minutes
Cooking   35 minutes
Total   55 minutes

EQUIPMENT:
Large saucepan
Saucepan
Whisk

INGREDIENTS:
½ cup unsalted butter
1 onion, diced
2 celery stalks, diced
2 carrots, diced
3 cups potato, diced
2 cup clam juice
1 tsp thyme
¼ cup all-purpose flour
2 cup half and half
2 cup shucked clams
1 lemon, juiced
salt, to taste
black pepper, to taste

INSTRUCTIONS:
1. Place a large saucepan on medium heat and ¼ cup butter.
2. Into the saucepan add the onion, celery, and carrot, cook for 10 minutes.
3. Then add the potatoes, clam juice and thyme, bring to a simmer and cook for 10 minutes.
4. Set a saucepan on medium heat and add the remaining butter.
5. Once melted, add all-purpose flour, and stir for 2 minutes to form a roux.
6. Gradually pour the half and half into the saucepan, whisking to combine into a smooth thick sauce.
7. Then add the thick creamy mixture to the saucepan of vegetables.
8. Stir the shucked clams into the saucepan and warm through for 2 minutes.
9. Taste the clam chowder and adjust the seasoning with lemon juice, salt, and black pepper.
10. Serve the clam chowder warm.

NEW ORLEANS GUMBO

SERVINGS: 4

TIME:
Preparation   15 minutes
Cooking   35 minutes
Total   50 minutes

EQUIPMENT:
Saucepan

INGREDIENTS:
1 tbsp vegetable oil
10 oz andouille sausage, sliced
1 tbsp all-purpose flour
1 onion, finely chopped
1 green bell pepper, finely chopped
4 celery stalks, finely chopped
2 clove garlic, finely chopped
2 cup chicken broth
3 tsp Cajun seasoning
½ tsp Worcestershire sauce
9 oz shrimp, peeled and deveined
¼ cup corn
1 tbsp parsley, finely chopped
salt, to taste
black pepper, to taste

INSTRUCTIONS:
1. Set a saucepan on medium heat and add the vegetable oil.
2. Place the sliced andouille sausage into the saucepan, cook for 3 minutes stirring occasionally until well browned.
3. Remove the andouille sausage from the saucepan and transfer to a plate.
4. Next add the flour to the saucepan, stir to form a thick paste and continue to cook for 10 minutes until a deep brown roux has formed.
5. Stir in the onion, green bell pepper, celery, and garlic, cook for 5 minutes.
6. Then add the chicken broth into the saucepan gradually, one ladle at a time. Stir the sauce to create a thick, smooth gravy and bring to a simmer.
7. Return the andouille sausage to the saucepan along with the Cajun seasoning, Worcestershire sauce, shrimp, and corn, cook for 5 minutes.
8. Season the New Orleans gumbo with parsley, salt and black pepper then serve.

FDNY Engine 299/Ladder 152 One Pan Baked Salmon and Vegetables

My last firehouse on Utopia Parkway in Queens. By this time, my books were published, and the cooking established, and I had learned to keep my "experiments" to previously tested recipes. Called "The Web" and although most firehouses in NYC were busy, some, like this had fewer calls. The older, experienced firefighters found it "boring" and complained, then got used to it. They were advised, once you get caught in "the web" there is no getting out, hence, the name! This recipe, a healthy one, I had made for the crew often.

SERVINGS: 4

TIME:
Preparation   15 minutes
Cooking   45 minutes
Total   1 hour

EQUIPMENT:
Mixing bowl x 2
Baking tray

INGREDIENTS:
2 cup new potato, halved
¼ cup olive oil
1 red onion, roughly chopped
10 oz asparagus, halved
1 lemon, juiced
1 tsp Dijon mustard
1 tsp honey
2 clove garlic, finely chopped
1 lb. salmon, sliced into 4 fillets
salt, to taste
black pepper, to taste

INSTRUCTIONS:
1. Preheat an oven to 400 degrees Fahrenheit and line a baking tray with aluminum foil, place the baking tray into the oven to preheat.
2. In a mixing bowl toss together the new potato, one tablespoon olive oil, salt, and black pepper.
3. Pour the potatoes onto the preheated baking tray and bake for 25 minutes.
4. In a bowl add the red onion, asparagus, one tablespoon olive oil, salt, and black pepper. Mix the ingredients with your hands to coat evenly then set aside.
5. Combine the lemon juice, Dijon mustard, honey, garlic, two tablespoons of olive oil, salt, and black pepper in a bowl.
6. Spoon the lemon and mustard dressing over the flesh-side of the salmon.
7. Remove the baking tray of potatoes from the oven after 25 minutes, to the tray add the asparagus, red onion and salmon, skin-side down.
8. Bake the salmon and vegetables in the oven for 15 minutes until cooked through.
9. Serve the baked salmon, asparagus, red onion, and potatoes hot.

SEAFOOD POT PIE

SERVINGS: 4

TIME:
Preparation   15 minutes
Cooking   45 minutes
Total   1 hour

EQUIPMENT:
Saucepan
Pie dish

INGREDIENTS:
1 tbsp vegetable oil
1 onion, diced
2 carrots, diced
2 celery stalks, diced
2 clove garlic, finely chopped
2 tsp Old Bay seasoning
¼ cup all-purpose flour
2 cup fish stock
1 cup potato, diced
½ cup heavy cream
1 lb. lump crab meat
1 lb. lobster meat, chopped
8 oz shrimp, peeled and deveined
6 scallops
1 cup frozen peas
1 cup corn
½ cup parsley, chopped
5 oz pie crust sheet
1 egg, lightly beaten
salt, to taste
black pepper, to taste

INSTRUCTIONS:
1. Place a saucepan on medium heat and add the vegetable oil.
2. Then add the onion, carrot, and celery, cook for 5 minutes.
3. Stir in the garlic and Old Bay seasoning, cook for 1 minute.
4. Next add the flour, stir for 1 minute to thicken.
5. Gradually pour the fish stock into the saucepan to create a thick, smooth sauce.
6. Then add the diced potato and bring the sauce to a simmer, cook for 10 minutes.
7. Stir the heavy cream, crab meat, lobster meat, shrimp, scallop, peas, corn, parsley, salt, and black pepper.
8. Transfer the seafood mixture to a pie dish and preheat an oven to 375 degrees Fahrenheit.
9. Lay the pie crust sheet over the pie tin and seal the edges.
10. Brush the pastry with lightly beaten egg and place the seafood pot pie in the oven.
11. Bake the seafood pot pie for 20 minutes until golden brown and bubbling.
12. Remove the seafood pot pie from the oven and allow it to rest for 5 minutes then serve hot.

SHRIMP BRUSCHETTA

Eggleston Volunteer FD

Eggleston, VA

I did a "celebrity chef appearance at the Paradise Restaurant in Eggleston, VA. The Paradise Restaurant is in the very small town of Eggleston, VA and was one of my best. The restaurant was made from an old hardware store and people come from far and wide due to its' reputation. I received tremendous response from both their chefs and attendees for this recipe as well as an honorary patch from the Eggleston Volunteer Fire Department.

SERVINGS: 4-6

TIME:
Preparation   20 minutes
Cooking   25 minutes
Total   45 minutes

EQUIPMENT:
Oven rack
Skillet

INGREDIENTS:
Toast
1 loaf ciabatta, cut into ¼" slices
1 tbsp olive oil
1 clove garlic, peeled

Shrimp
1 shallot, thinly sliced
2 cloves garlic, finely chopped
1 lb. large shrimp, peeled and deveined
6 Roma tomatoes, chopped
⅓ cup white wine
¼ cup chicken broth
3 tbsp tarragon, finely chopped
1 cup arugula, chopped
½ cup mascarpone cheese, room temperature
salt, to taste
black pepper, to taste

INSTRUCTIONS:
1. Preheat an oven to 400 degrees Fahrenheit and place an oven rack into the center of the oven.
2. Drizzle the ciabatta slices with olive oil then transfer to the oven rack.
3. Bake the ciabatta for 10 minutes until toasted, remove from the oven and allow to cool for 2 minutes.
4. Rub the warm ciabatta with a clove of peeled garlic, set aside.
5. Place a skillet on medium heat and add the olive oil.
6. Then add the shallot and garlic, stir to soften for 2 minutes.
7. Next add the shrimp to the skillet, season with salt and black pepper.
8. Cook the shrimp for 4 minutes then remove from the skillet, cut into ½" pieces and set aside.
9. Place the skillet back on the stove and add the chopped tomatoes, cook for 4 minutes to soften.
10. Increase the heat to high and pour in the wine, deglaze the base of the skillet.
11. Reduce the wine by half then add the chicken broth, simmer for 2 minutes.
12. Remove the skillet from the stove and add the tarragon, arugula, mascarpone, cooked shrimp, salt, and black pepper.
13. Stir until the mixture is creamy and come together.
14. Top each toasted ciabatta with the shrimp mixture and serve.

CHICKEN

Lt. Nicholas Reale Pinellas Park FD and Sal Reale FDNY at the World Trade Center Museum in front of Ladder 3. I was at that very firehouse doing a live television cooking segment for WB 11 TV the morning of 9/11/01. See story and video on website www.americanfirehousecuisine.com

REALE CHICKEN PARMIGIANA

SERVINGS: 4

TIME:

Preparation   15 minutes
Cooking   45 minutes
Total   1 hour

EQUIPMENT:

Saucepan
Mixing bowl x 3
Sauté pan
Baking tray

INGREDIENTS:

Sauce

1 tbsp olive oil
1 onion, finely chopped
2 cloves garlic, finely chopped
½ tsp red pepper flakes
28 oz canned crushed tomatoes
1 tsp dried Italian herbs

Chicken

4 chicken breasts
2 cups all-purpose flour
3 eggs, lightly beaten
2 cups breadcrumbs
salt, to taste
black pepper, to taste
1 tbsp olive oil
3 cups mozzarella, shredded
1 cup parmesan cheese, grated

Lt. Nick Reale
Pinellas Park Fire Department
Pinellas Park, FL
Sal Reale FDNY
In Memory of Thomas Reale
Tampa FD Tampa, FL

I met Nick at a cooking demonstration with the Mayor of Tampa. Nick and his father Sal (retired FDNY) approached me after the event. Nick also designed websites and asked if I had one. I did but a basic one and Nick helped me develop a terrific website which led to many opportunities. We had much in common, a father who was in the FDNY and a brother who was a firefighter. I found out later in conversation, that when I published my first cookbook, *The Healthy Firehouse Cookbook*, Nick had sent a recipe when I had placed an ad in *Firehouse Magazine*. I never used it but to make it up to him, here is his recipe, 28 years later! Nick has retired and pursues several interests, website design www. cappuccinomediagroup.com and is quite the woodworker, turning bowls from rare woods www.nickrealewoodturning.com.

INSTRUCTIONS:

Sauce

1. Place a saucepan on medium heat and add the olive oil.
2. Stir the onion into the saucepan, cook for 3 minutes to soften.
3. Then add the garlic and red pepper flakes, cook for 1 minute until fragrant.
4. Pour the crushed tomatoes into the saucepan, bring to a simmer, and cook for 15 minutes.
5. Remove the sauce from the heat and allow it to cool, season with Italian herbs, salt, and black pepper.

Chicken

1. Preheat an oven to 400 degrees Fahrenheit.
2. Slice the chicken breasts through the middle lengthways, without cutting all the way through the meat. Cover the chicken with a sheet of plastic wrap and bat out into ½" thickness.
3. Into three separate mixing bowls add the flour, eggs and breadcrumbs, season each with salt and black pepper.
4. Dip the chicken breasts into the bowl of flour, then into the egg, then into the breadcrumb and place on a plate, repeat for each chicken breast.
5. Place a sauté pan on medium heat and add the olive oil.
6. Fry the breaded chicken in the sauté pan for 3 minutes then flip and cook for a further 3 minutes.
7. Transfer the breaded chicken to a baking tray and top each with a generous amount of tomato sauce, shredded mozzarella, and parmesan cheese.
8. Bake the chicken parmigiana in the preheated oven for 15 minutes then serve.

Chicken Pot Pie

SERVINGS: 8

TIME:
Preparation   20 minutes
Cooking   1 hour
Total   1 hour 20 minutes

EQUIPMENT:
Saucepan
9" Pie dish
Rolling pin

INGREDIENTS:
1 pre-made pie shell
1 pre-made pie crust
4 cups cooked chicken, shredded
¼ cup unsalted butter
1 onion, finely chopped
2 carrots, thinly sliced
1 celery stalks, thinly sliced
2 cups mushroom, thinly sliced
2 cloves garlic, finely chopped
5 tbsp all-purpose flour
2 cups chicken broth
½ cup heavy cream
1 cup frozen peas
2 tbsp parsley, finely chopped
1 egg, lightly beaten
salt, to taste
black pepper, to taste

INSTRUCTIONS:
1. Preheat an oven to 425F and place a pie shell in a pie tin.
2. Place a saucepan on medium heat and add the butter.
3. Then add the onion, carrot, and celery, cook for 5 minutes to soften.
4. Next add the mushroom and garlic, cook for 3 minutes.
5. Stir the flour into the saucepan, cook out for 2 minutes.
6. Pour the chicken broth into the saucepan and mix to form a smooth sauce.
7. Then add the heavy cream, salt and black pepper, season to taste.
8. Remove the saucepan from the stove and add the shredded chicken, peas, and parsley.
9. Pour the chicken mixture into the pre-made pie shell then roll the pie crust to 10" wide.
10. Place the pie crust over the pie base and crimp the edges with a fork.
11. Brush the surface of the pie with a lightly beaten egg then bake in the preheated oven for 30 minutes.
12. Once the chicken pot pie is golden brown, remove from the oven and allow it to cool for 15 minutes before serving.

Chicken Noodle Soup

SERVINGS: 4-6

TIME:
Preparation   20 minutes
Cooking   20 minutes
Total   40 minutes

EQUIPMENT:
Saucepan

INGREDIENTS:
1 tbsp unsalted butter
2 carrots, finely chopped
1 onion, finely chopped
2 celery stalks, finely chopped
2 cups mushroom, thinly sliced
8 cups chicken broth
1 tsp thyme leaves
1 lb. cooked chicken breast, diced
6 oz egg noodles
salt, to taste
black pepper, to taste

INSTRUCTIONS:
1. Place a saucepan on medium heat and add the butter.
2. Then add the carrot, onion, and celery, cook for 5 minutes.
3. Next add the sliced mushrooms and cook for 5 minutes.
4. Pour the chicken broth into the saucepan and bring to a boil, season with salt.
5. When the broth is boiling, stir in the egg noodles and cook for 5 minutes.
6. Then add the thyme leaves and chicken breast, warm the chicken for 5 minutes.
7. Season the chicken noodle soup with salt and black pepper then serve hot.

ORANGE CHICKEN

SERVINGS: 4

TIME:
Preparation   20 minutes
Cooking   30 minutes
Total   50 minutes

EQUIPMENT:
Mixing bowl x 2
Whisk
Saucepan
Sauté pan / Wok

INGREDIENTS:
Chicken
4 chicken breasts, diced into ¼" pieces
2 tbsp orange juice
2 eggs, lightly beaten
½ cup cornstarch
2 cups canola oil

Sauce
1 tsp sesame oil
1-inch ginger, finely chopped
2 cloves garlic, finely chopped
¼ cup orange juice
¼ cup soy sauce
¼ cup brown sugar
2 tbsp rice vinegar
1 tbsp cornstarch
6 scallions, thinly sliced

INSTRUCTIONS:
Chicken
1. In a bowl add the diced chicken, two tablespoons orange juice, salt, and black pepper.
2. Stir to combine then place the bowl in the refrigerator to marinate for 20 minutes.
3. In a separate bowl whisk the eggs and cornstarch to form a smooth batter.
4. Fold the chicken into the bowl of batter to coat completely.
5. Place a saucepan on medium heat and add the canola oil, preheat to 360F.
6. Fry the chicken in batches in batches in the preheated oil until crisp, approximately 3 minutes.
7. Remove the chicken from the pan and transfer to a plate lined with kitchen paper.
8. Increase the temperature of the oil to 390 degrees Fahrenheit and fry the chicken for a second time for 3 minutes until golden brown and crisp.

Sauce
1. Place a sauté pan on medium heat and add the sesame oil.
2. Stir the ginger and garlic into the pan, cook for 1 minute.
3. Pour the orange juice, soy sauce and brown sugar, bring to a simmer.
4. In a bowl stir together the rice vinegar and cornstarch.
5. Whisk the rice vinegar and cornstarch into the pan, stirring continuously to form a thick, smooth sauce.
6. Remove the orange sauce from the heat and stir in the crispy chicken.
7. Transfer the orange chicken to a dish and serve, topped with scallions.

CHICKEN AND DUMPLINGS

SERVINGS: 4

TIME:
Preparation   30 minutes
Cooking   1 hour
Total   1 hour 30 minutes

EQUIPMENT:
Saucepan with a lid
Mixing bowl

INGREDIENTS:

Chicken
2 tbsp unsalted butter
1 cup onion, chopped
1 cup celery, chopped
1 cup carrot, chopped
2 cloves garlic, finely chopped
¼ cup white wine
¼ cup all-purpose flour
4 cups chicken broth
2 cups cooked chicken, shredded
1 tsp dried thyme
1 tbsp parsley, finely chopped

DUMPLINGS
1 cup all-purpose flour
2 tsp baking powder
2 tbsp parsley, finely chopped
1 tbsp chives, finely chopped
⅔ cup milk
salt, to taste
black pepper, to taste

INSTRUCTIONS:

Chicken
1. Place a saucepan on medium heat and add butter.
2. Then add the onion, celery, and carrot, cook for 5 minutes.
3. Next add the garlic, cook for 1 minute until fragrant.
4. Pour white wine in the saucepan, bring to a boil, and reduce by half.
5. Stir the flour through the saucepan, cook out for 2 minutes.
6. Gradually add the chicken broth to the saucepan to form a thick and smooth sauce.
7. Fold the shredded chicken, thyme and parsley into the saucepan, season with salt and black pepper.
8. Reduce the heat of the saucepan to low and prepare the dumplings.

Dumplings
1. In a mixing bowl stir together the flour, baking powder, parsley, chives, salt, and black pepper.
2. Pour the milk into the mixing bowl and mix to create a loose dough.
3. Spoon heaped tablespoons of the dough onto the surface of the chicken mixture.
4. Place a lid on the saucepan and cook for 10 minutes.
5. Once the dumplings are plump and tender, serve the chicken and dumplings.

CHICKEN FRIED STEAK

SERVINGS: 4

TIME:
Preparation   25 minutes
Cooking   20 minutes
Total   45 minutes

EQUIPMENT:
Meat mallet
Mixing bowl x 2
Skillet
Wire cooling rack

INGREDIENTS:
4 x 6 oz round steaks
1 ½ cups all-purpose flour
2 tsp garlic powder
1 tsp onion powder
½ tsp cayenne pepper
2 eggs, lightly beaten
½ cup milk
salt, to taste
black pepper, to taste
1 cup canola oil

INSTRUCTIONS:
1. Place the round steak on a chopping board and cover with plastic wrap.
2. Use a meat mallet to tenderize the steaks and bat out into ¼-inch thickness.
3. Into a mixing bowl add the flour, garlic powder, onion powder, cayenne pepper, salt, and black pepper.
4. In a separate bowl whisk the eggs, milk, salt, and black pepper.
5. Place a steak into the bowl of flour then transfer to the bowl of egg, return to the bowl of flour, and press to tightly pack the flour into the meat.
6. Repeat to flour all the steaks.
7. Place a skillet on medium heat and add the canola oil, preheat to 320F.
8. Lay the floured steaks into the skillet and cook for 4 minutes then flip the steak and cook for a further 4 minutes.
9. Once the chicken fried steaks are golden brown remove from the skillet and allow to drain on a wire rack for 5 minutes before serving.

CHICKEN SALAD

SERVINGS: 4

TIME:
Preparation   20 minutes
Total   20 minutes

EQUIPMENT:
Mixing bowl

INGREDIENTS:
2 cups cooked chicken, shredded
½ cup mayonnaise
2 celery stalks, chopped
6 scallions, thinly sliced
2 tbsp parsley, finely chopped
1 tbsp lemon juice
1 tsp Dijon mustard
black pepper, to taste

INSTRUCTIONS:
1. In a mixing bowl add the shredded chicken, mayonnaise, celery, scallions, parsley, lemon juice, Dijon mustard and black pepper.
2. Stir the chicken salad to combine.
3. Refrigerate the salad to allow the flavors to come together and chill before serving.

BLACKENED CHICKEN

SERVINGS: 4

TIME:
Preparation 15 minutes
Cooking 15 minutes
Total 30 minutes

EQUIPMENT:
Saucepan
Sauté pan

INGREDIENTS:
½ cup unsalted butter
1 tbsp smoked paprika
1 tbsp ground cumin
1 tbsp garlic powder
1 tbsp onion powder
2 tsp dried thyme
4 chicken breasts
salt, to taste
black pepper, to taste
¼ cup cilantro, finely chopped
1 lime, juiced

INSTRUCTIONS:
1. Place a saucepan on low heat and add ¼ cup of butter.
2. Melt the butter then whisk in smoked paprika, ground cumin, garlic powder, onion powder, dried thyme, salt, and black pepper.
3. Cook the spices for 30 seconds until a thick, dark paste then remove from the heat.
4. Brush the blackened paste over the surface of each chicken breast.
5. Place a sauté pan on medium heat and add the remaining butter.
6. Lay the blackened chicken breasts into the sauté pan, sear for 5 minutes.
7. Flip the chicken and cook for a further 5 minutes.
8. Then remove the chicken from the pan and allow it to rest for 5 minutes.
9. Serve the blackened chicken topped with cilantro and a squeeze of fresh lime juice.

CHICKEN CASSERINOROLE

SERVINGS: 6

TIME:
Preparation   20 minutes
Cooking   30 minutes
Total   50 minutes

EQUIPMENT:
Casserole dish
Mixing bowl x 2

INGREDIENTS:
3 chicken breasts, diced
1 tbsp smoked paprika
2 tsp garlic powder
2 tsp onion powder
3 oz cooked bacon, diced
1 cup cream cheese, softened
1 cup sour cream
1 tbsp parsley, finely chopped
½ cup Monterey Jack, shredded
salt, to taste
black pepper, to taste

In honor of my Lindenhurst, NY high school friend, Frank Casserino, who went to the United States Air Force Academy, worked in the Space Program, and went on to be a two-star General in the USAF.

Casseroles are great in firehouses or at home! Not only a good use of leftovers but as a firehouse cook, anything we can make in large quantities and all in one pan worked well. Easier to cook and reheat if called out to an alarm in the middle of cooking.

INSTRUCTIONS:
1. Preheat an oven to 375 degrees Fahrenheit.
2. In a bowl add the diced chicken, smoked paprika, garlic, onion powder, salt, and black pepper.
3. Place the chicken into the base of a casserole dish.
4. In a separate bowl fold together the bacon, cream cheese, sour cream, and parsley.
5. Spread the cheese mixture over the chicken into an even layer, then top the casserole with shredded cheese.
6. Transfer the chicken casserole for 30 minutes, until golden brown and the chicken is cooked through.

BBQ Chicken Wings

SERVINGS: 4

TIME:
Preparation   15 minutes
Cooking   1 hour
Total   1 hour 15 minutes

EQUIPMENT:
Mixing bowl
Baking tray
Saucepan

INGREDIENTS:
2 lb. chicken wing
2 tbsp canola oil
2 tbsp all-purpose flour
1 tsp garlic powder
1 tsp cayenne pepper
1 tsp smoked paprika
¼ tsp salt
½ cup BBQ sauce
¼ cup honey
2 tbsp hot sauce (optional)

INSTRUCTIONS:
1. Preheat an oven to 440F and line a baking tray with parchment paper.
2. Into a mixing bowl add the chicken wings, canola oil, flour, garlic powder, cayenne pepper, paprika and salt.
3. Place the chicken wings onto the baking tray and transfer to the oven.
4. Bake for 40 minutes until crisp and golden, turn halfway through cooking.
5. Place a saucepan on low heat and add the BBQ sauce, honey, and hot sauce.
6. Bring the BBQ sauce to a simmer then remove from the heat.
7. After 40 minutes of baking, remove the wings from the oven and brush with BBQ sauce to cover.
8. Place the BBQ chicken wings back into the oven and bake for a further 10 minutes until sticky and glazed.

GENERAL TSO'S CHICKEN

SERVINGS: 4

TIME:
Preparation   20 minutes
Cooking   30 minutes
Total   50 minutes

EQUIPMENT:
Mixing bowl
Saucepan
Whisk
Sauté pan / Wok

INGREDIENTS:

Chicken
6 chicken thighs, diced
2 tsp soy sauce
1 egg yolk
salt, to taste
black pepper, to taste
½ cup cornstarch
½ cup all-purpose flour
2 cups canola oil

Sauce
1 tsp sesame oil
1-inch ginger, finely chopped
2 cloves garlic, finely chopped
8 dried red chilies, chopped
¼ cup brown sugar
2 tbsp Chinese black vinegar
3 tbsp soy sauce
2 tsp chili paste
2 tsp cornstarch
½ cup chicken broth
2 tbsp sesame seeds

INSTRUCTIONS:

Chicken
1. In a mixing bowl add the chicken thigh, soy sauce, egg yolk, salt, and black pepper.
2. Stir the chicken to coat then allow to marinade for 15 minutes.
3. Then add the cornstarch and all-purpose flour to the mixing bowl, toss the chicken through the flour to coat.
4. Remove the chicken thigh from the flour and shake off the excess.
5. Place a saucepan on medium heat and add canola oil, preheat to 390 degrees FahrenheitF.
6. In batches, fry the floured chicken for 3 minutes stirring occasionally to prevent sticking.
7. Remove the fried chicken from the oil and drain on a plate lined with kitchen paper, set aside.

Sauce
1. In a bowl whisk together the brown sugar, Chinese black vinegar, soy sauce, chili paste, cornstarch, and chicken broth.
2. Place a sauté pan on medium heat and add the sesame oil.
3. Then add the ginger, garlic, and red chili, cook for 30 seconds.
4. Pour the prepared sauce into the sauté pan and bring to a simmer.
5. Cook the sauce for 2 minutes, stirring to form a smooth, thick consistency.
6. Next add the crispy chicken to the pan of sauce and toss to coat.
7. Transfer the General Tso's chicken to a serving platter and garnish with sesame seeds.

KENTUCKY FRIED CHICKEN

SERVINGS: 4

TIME:
Preparation   20 minutes
Marinade   6 hours
Cooking   25 minutes
Total   6 hours 45 minutes

EQUIPMENT:
Mixing bowl x 2
Saucepan
Wire cooling rack
Meat thermometer

INGREDIENTS:
8 chicken thigh / drumsticks
2 cups buttermilk
4 tsp paprika
3 tsp ground white pepper
2 tsp garlic powder
1 tsp ground ginger
1 tsp mustard powder
1 tsp celery salt
1 tsp ground black pepper
½ tsp dried thyme
½ tsp dried oregano
1 tsp salt
2 cups all-purpose flour
½ cup cornstarch
4 cups canola oil

INSTRUCTIONS:
1. In a bowl mix the paprika, white pepper, garlic powder, ground ginger, mustard powder, celery salt, black pepper, thyme, oregano, and salt to form the spice mix.
2. Into a mixing bowl add the buttermilk and half the spice mix, stir to combine.
3. Then add the chicken pieces and cover the bowl, refrigerate for at least 6 hours to marinate the chicken.
4. In a second mixing bowl add the all-purpose flour, cornstarch, and remaining spice mix.
5. Once the chicken has marinated, remove the pieces from the buttermilk and shake off the excess, place the chicken into the bowl of flour and allow it to sit for 5 minutes.
6. Place a saucepan on medium heat and add the canola oil, preheat to 400 degrees Fahrenheit.
7. In batches, add the breaded chicken to the preheated oil and cook for 8 minutes until crisp and golden brown.
8. Check the internal temperature of the chicken with a meat thermometer, it should reach 175F.
9. Transfer the Kentucky Fried Chicken to a wire cooling rack and continue to fry the chicken in batches until all is cooked.

RICE/POTATO/ PASTA

MACARONI AND CHEESE

SERVINGS: 6-8

TIME:
Preparation   20 minutes
Cooking   1 hour
Total   1 hour 20 minutes

EQUIPMENT:
Saucepan x 2
Whisk
Mixing bowl
9"x13" baking dish

INGREDIENTS:
¼ cup unsalted butter
¼ cup all-purpose flour
4 cups milk
½ cup Gruyere cheese, grated
1 cup cheddar cheese, grated
1 cup mozzarella cheese, shredded
1 tbsp Dijon mustard
1 cup parmesan cheese, grated
1 lb. macaroni pasta
salt, to taste
black pepper, to taste

INSTRUCTIONS:
1. Preheat an oven to 375 degrees Fahrenheit.
2. Place a large saucepan on medium heat and add the butter.
3. Melt the butter then stir in the flour, whisk for 2 minutes to cook out the flour.
4. Gradually pour the milk into the saucepan, continuing to whisk to form a thick, smooth bechamel sauce.
5. In a mixing bowl add the Gruyere cheese, cheddar cheese, mozzarella cheese, Dijon mustard and ½ cup parmesan, pour the saucepan of bechamel sauce into the mixing bowl and fold together to melt the cheese.
6. Fill a separate saucepan with water, season with salt and place on a high heat.
7. Bring the water to a boil and cook the pasta for 6 minutes until al dente.
8. Transfer the cooked pasta into the cheese sauce, mix to combine.
9. Then add the macaroni and cheese to a baking dish, top with the remaining grated parmesan.
10. Place the baking dish in the preheated oven for 35 minutes until golden brown and bubbling.
11. Allow the macaroni and cheese to rest for 10 minutes before serving.

PENNE ALLA VODKA

SERVINGS: 4

TIME:
Preparation   15 minutes
Cooking   20 minutes
Total   35 minutes

EQUIPMENT:
Saucepan x 2
Blender
Colander

INGREDIENTS:
¼ cup olive oil
1 onion, finely chopped
6 cloves garlic, thinly sliced
1 tsp red chili flakes
4 oz tomato paste
¼ cup vodka
1 cup heavy cream
1 lb. penne pasta
1 cup parmesan cheese, grated
black pepper, to taste
salt, to taste

INSTRUCTIONS:
1. Place a large saucepan on medium heat and add the olive oil.
2. Once the oil is shimmering, add the onion and cook for 5 minutes to soften.
3. Then add garlic and chili flakes, cook for 2 minutes until lightly browned.
4. Next stir in the tomato paste, continue to stir for 3 minutes until the paste becomes a deep red.
5. Pour the vodka into the saucepan and bring to a boil, reduce the vodka, and stir to deglaze the saucepan.
6. Gradually add the heavy cream to the saucepan, stir to combine then remove the saucepan from the heat.
7. Fill a second saucepan with water, season generously with salt and place on a high heat.
8. When the water is boiling, add the penne pasta and cook for 8 minutes.
9. Reserve one cup of pasta cooking water then strain the pasta through a colander.
10. Transfer the cooked pasta and pasta water to the saucepan of vodka sauce, stir to combine.
11. Gradually fold in the parmesan cheese then serve the dish hot, season with freshly cracked black pepper.

CHICKEN ALFREDO

SERVINGS: 6

TIME:
Preparation   20 minutes
Cooking   30 minutes
Total   50 minutes

EQUIPMENT:
Saucepan x 2
Grater

INGREDIENTS:
1 lb. chicken thigh, roughly chopped
3 clove garlic, finely chopped
1 tsp thyme
1 tbsp olive oil
1 lb. fettuccine pasta
2 tbsp unsalted butter
1 onion, finely chopped
1 lb. button mushroom, sliced
2 cups heavy cream
1 cup parmesan cheese, grated
1 tbsp parsley, finely chopped
salt, to taste
black pepper, to taste

INSTRUCTIONS:
1. Into a bowl add the chicken thigh, one clove of chopped garlic, thyme, salt, and black pepper.
2. Place a saucepan on medium heat and add the olive oil.
3. Then add the seasoned chicken to the pan, cook for 5 minutes to sear, transfer the chicken to a plate and set aside.
4. Next add the butter into the saucepan.
5. Once the butter has melted, add the onion and mushroom, cook for 5 minutes.
6. Stir in the remaining garlic, cook for 1 minute until fragrant.
7. Then pour the heavy cream into the pan, bring to a simmer, and reduce for 10 minutes.
8. Fill a separate saucepan with water, season with salt and place on a high heat.
9. Bring the water to a boil and cook the pasta for 8 minutes until al dente.
10. Transfer the cooked pasta into the alfredo sauce along with the seared chicken, parmesan, parsley, salt, and black pepper.
11. Fold the ingredients together for 2 minutes to warm through then serve the chicken alfredo hot.

BAKED ZITI

SERVINGS: 6

TIME:
Preparation   15 minutes
Cooking   1 hour 15 minutes
Total   1 hour 30 minutes

EQUIPMENT:
Saucepan x 2
Mixing bowl
9"x13" baking dish

INGREDIENTS:
¼ cup olive oil
1 onion, finely chopped
2 cloves garlic, thinly sliced
1 tbsp tomato paste
28 oz canned tomatoes
2 tsp oregano, finely chopped
¼ cup unsalted butter
1 lb. ziti pasta
1 lb. ricotta cheese
1 cup mozzarella, shredded
½ cup heavy cream
½ cup parmesan cheese, grated
1 cup breadcrumbs
salt, to taste
black pepper, to taste

INSTRUCTIONS:
1. Place a saucepan on medium heat and add the olive oil.
2. Stir in the onion and garlic, cook for 5 minutes to soften.
3. Then add the tomato paste, cook out for 2 minutes.
4. Pour the canned tomatoes and butter into the saucepan, season with oregano, salt, and black pepper.
5. Reduce the sauce to a simmer, cook for 20 minutes.
6. Fill a saucepan with water, season with salt and place on a high heat.
7. Bring the water to a boil then add the ziti pasta, cook for 5 minutes then strain.
8. Transfer the pasta to the saucepan of tomato sauce, remove from the stove.
9. In a mixing bowl combine the ricotta cheese, mozzarella cheese, heavy cream, and parmesan.
10. Preheat an oven to 425 degrees Fahrenheit
11. Into the baking dish add ⅓ of the pasta mixture and spread to an even layer.
12. Next add a ⅓ of the cheese mixture, continue to layer with pasta and cheese until the ingredients have been used.
13. Top the baked ziti with breadcrumbs then place in the preheated oven.
14. Bake for 35 minutes until golden brown and bubbling.

CHICKEN RIGGIES

SERVINGS: 6

TIME:
Preparation   15 minutes
Cooking   30 minutes
Total   45 minutes

EQUIPMENT:
Saucepan x 2

INGREDIENTS:
1 tbsp olive oil
1 onion, finely chopped
1 tsp garlic, finely chopped
1 tsp chili flakes
3 oz white wine
2 sweet red peppers, roasted and chopped
28 oz canned fire roasted tomato
½ cup heavy cream
½ rotisserie chicken, meat shredded
1 tsp basil, finely chopped
½ tsp oregano, finely chopped
1 lb. rigatoni
1 cup parmesan cheese, grated
¼ cup jarred pickled chilies, roughly chopped
(jalapeno, guindillas, cherry peppers, Calabrian)

INSTRUCTIONS:
1. Place a saucepan on medium heat and add the olive oil.
2. Then add the onion to the saucepan, cook for 5 minutes.
3. Stir in the chili flakes, cook for 1 minute until fragrant.
4. Pour the white wine into the saucepan, reduce by half.
5. Next add the sweet red pepper, fire roasted tomatoes, heavy cream, rotisserie chicken, basil, and oregano.
6. Reduce the heat to low and cook the sauce for 20 minutes.
7. Fill a second saucepan with water and season with salt. Place the saucepan on high heat and bring to a boil.
8. Once boiling, add the pasta to the water and cook for 8 minutes.
9. Transfer the al dente pasta to the saucepan of sauce, stir in the parmesan cheese and allow to come together for 1 minute.
10. Serve the chicken riggies topped with chopped pickled chilies.

Potato Salad

SERVINGS: 8

TIME:
Preparation   25 minutes
Cooking   15 minutes
Total   40 minutes

EQUIPMENT:
Saucepan
Mixing bowl

INGREDIENTS:
3 lb. red potatoes, washed
1 red onion, finely chopped
2 celery stalks, finely chopped
4 dill pickles, finely chopped
2 tbsp parsley, finely chopped
1 cup mayonnaise
⅓ cup Dijon mustard
1 tbsp apple cider vinegar
½ tsp garlic powder
½ tsp smoked paprika
salt, to taste
black pepper, to taste

INSTRUCTIONS:
1. Into a saucepan add the potatoes then cover with water and season with salt.
2. Place the saucepan on medium heat and bring to a boil.
3. Reduce the saucepan to a simmer and cook the potatoes for 15 minutes until tender.
4. Strain the potatoes through a colander and allow to cool for 5 minutes.
5. Whilst still warm, peel the skin using a cloth then roughly chop the potatoes and add to a mixing bowl.
6. Into the mixing bowl add the red onion, celery, pickles, and parsley.
7. In a separate bowl stir together the mayonnaise, Dijon mustard, apple cider vinegar, garlic powder, smoked paprika, salt, and black pepper.
8. Gently fold the mayonnaise mixture into the potato salad to combine then place the bowl in the refrigerator to chill.
9. Serve the potato salad chilled, best after a few hours in the refrigerator.

STUFFED BAKED POTATOES

SERVINGS: 8

TIME:
Preparation   30 minutes
Cooking   1 hour
Total   1 hour 30 minutes

EQUIPMENT:
Baking tray
Mixing bowl

INGREDIENTS:
1 tbsp canola oil
8 large russet potatoes, washed
¼ cup unsalted butter, diced
1 cup sour cream
1 cup Monterey Jack cheese
8 oz bacon, cooked and chopped
salt, to taste
black pepper, to taste

INSTRUCTIONS:
1. Preheat an oven to 400 degrees Fahrenheit and line a baking tray with parchment paper.
2. Rub the potatoes with canola oil then season with salt and place on the baking tray.
3. Bake the potatoes for 40 minutes until tender.
4. Allow the potatoes to cool at room temperature for 10 minutes then slice in half lengthways.
5. Scoop the flesh from the inside of the potato leaving a thin rim between the skin.
6. Into a mixing bowl add the potato flesh, butter, sour cream, half a cup of Monterey Jack cheese, scallions, bacon, salt, and black pepper.
7. Fill the potato skins with the mashed potato filling then return to a baking sheet.
8. Scatter the remaining Monterey Jack cheese over each stuffed baked potato then place in the oven for 20 minutes until crisp and golden brown.
9. Serve a stuffed baked potato per person.

COUGZILLA MASHED POTATOES

Thomas Coughlin
FDNY Ladder 129

Spent many years with Tom from his first day in Ladder 129 and saw me go from lousy cook to cookbook author! He has been on a few television shows with me and has now retired, in good health near me in Indian Rocks Beach, FL. Cougzilla is my nickname for his son Alex, now a professional wrestler!

SERVINGS: 8

TIME:
Preparation   20 minutes
Cooking   1 hour 15 minutes
Total   45 minutes

EQUIPMENT:
Sauté pan
Saucepan
Colander
Masher
9"x13" baking dish

INGREDIENTS:
5 lb. russet potatoes, peeled and roughly chopped
6 slices bacon
1 cup unsalted butter
1 cup half-and-half
½ cup sour cream
2 cloves garlic, grated
6 scallions, thinly sliced
2 cups Monterey Jack cheese, shredded
salt, to taste
black pepper, to taste

INSTRUCTIONS:
1. Fill a saucepan with the potatoes and cover with water, season with salt.
2. Place the saucepan over a medium heat and bring to a boil, reduce the heat to a simmer and cook the potatoes for 20 minutes until tender.
3. Meanwhile, place a sauté pan on medium heat and add the bacon.
4. Fry the bacon for 3 minutes then flip and cook for a further 3 minutes until crispy, transfer the bacon to a plate to cool then roughly chop.
5. Once the potatoes are cooked, strain through a colander and allow to steam dry for 5 minutes.
6. Return the potatoes to the dry saucepan and crush with a potato masher then add the butter.
7. Next add the half-and-half and the sour cream, continue to mash to create a smooth consistency.
8. Into the mashed potatoes fold the grated garlic, scallions, chopped bacon, one cup of shredded cheese, salt, and black pepper.
9. Preheat an oven to 350 degrees Fahrenheit and transfer the loaded mashed potato into a baking dish.
10. Scatter the remaining Monterey Jack cheese over the mashed potato and bake for 20 minutes until melted and golden brown.

VEGETABLE FRIED RICE

SERVINGS: 4

TIME:
Preparation   15 minutes
Cooking   15 minutes
Total   30 minutes

EQUIPMENT:
Sauté pan

INGREDIENTS:
1 tbsp sesame oil
1 clove garlic, thinly sliced
1 tbsp ginger, thinly sliced
1 carrot, thinly sliced
4 oz baby corn
6 oz baby broccoli
1 cup beansprouts
1 cup cooked rice, chilled
2 scallions, thinly sliced
1 tsp light soy sauce
1 tbsp lime juice
2 tsp sesame seeds
¼ cup peanuts, roughly chopped
¼ cup cilantro, roughly chopped

INSTRUCTIONS:
1. Place a sauté pan on high heat and add the sesame oil.
2. Then add the garlic and ginger, cook for 30 seconds.
3. Next add the carrot, baby corn, baby broccoli and beansprouts, cook for 2 minutes stirring regularly.
4. Stir in the rice, use a spatula to break up the grains of rice and toast in the pan.
5. Scatter the scallions into the rice, season with light soy sauce and lime juice.
6. Transfer the vegetable fried rice to a plate to serve, top with sesame seeds, peanuts, and cilantro.

PASTA IL POMPIERE

SERVINGS: 6-8

TIME:
Preparation   15 minutes
Cooking   15 minutes
Total   30 minutes

EQUIPMENT:
Sauté pan
Saucepan
Colander

INGREDIENTS:
½ cup extra virgin olive oil
6 cloves garlic, thinly sliced
8 ripe plum tomatoes, roughly chopped
8 oz mozzarella cheese, shredded
½ tsp salt
2 cups arugula
1 lb. penne pasta
1 cup parmesan cheese, grated
dried red pepper flakes, to taste

INSTRUCTIONS:
1. Place a sauté pan on medium heat and add the olive oil.
2. Stir the sliced garlic into the sauté pan, cook for 2 minutes until golden and toasted.
3. Remove the garlic from the stove.
4. Into a mixing bowl add the garlic, chopped tomatoes, mozzarella cheese, salt and one cup of arugula, toss to combine.
5. Fill a saucepan with water and place on high heat, season with salt.
6. Bring the water to a boil then add the penne pasta, cook for 8 minutes.
7. Drain the pasta through a colander then add the mixing bowl of tomatoes.
8. Serve the pasta il pompiere topped with remaining arugula, grated parmesan, and red pepper flakes.

74

VEGETABLES

WALDORF SALAD

SERVINGS: 4

TIME:
Preparation   20 minutes
Total   20 minutes

EQUIPMENT:
Mixing bowl

INGREDIENTS:
⅓ cup mayonnaise
¼ cup sour cream
2 tbsp lemon juice
1 tbsp tarragon, finely chopped
3 green apples, cored and diced
1 cup mixed grapes, halved
1 cup celeriac, diced
1 cup walnuts, toasted and chopped
salt, to taste
black pepper, to taste

INSTRUCTIONS:
1. In a mixing bowl whisk together mayonnaise, sour cream, lemon juice, tarragon, salt, and black pepper.
2. Then add the diced apple, grapes, celeriac, and walnuts.
3. Toss the ingredients through the dressing to coat evenly.
4. Serve the Waldorf salad immediately or chill and use as a side dish.

Broccoli-Cauliflower Mash

SERVINGS: 8

TIME:
Preparation   20 minutes
Cooking   10 minutes
Total   30 minutes

EQUIPMENT:
Saucepan with a lid
Steamer basket
Potato masher

INGREDIENTS:
4 cups cauliflower florets
2 cups broccoli florets
1 tbsp olive oil
2 clove garlic, finely chopped
2 tsp thyme, picked
2 tsp rosemary, picked and chopped
1 tbsp parsley, finely chopped
½ cup unsalted butter
salt, to taste
black pepper, to taste

INSTRUCTIONS:
1. Fill a saucepan with 2-inches of water and place on high heat.
2. Bring the water to a boil then insert a steamer basket into the saucepan.
3. Place the cauliflower and broccoli florets into the steamer basket and cover with a lid, steam for 5 minutes.
4. Remove the cauliflower and broccoli florets from the steamer basket and add to a mixing bowl.
5. Place a sauté pan on medium heat and add the olive oil.
6. Stir the garlic, rosemary, and thyme into the sauté pan, cook for 1 minute.
7. Then add the garlic and herbs to the steamed florets along with the parsley, butter, salt, and black pepper.
8. Use a potato masher to crush the florets into a smooth mash.
9. Serve the broccoli-cauliflower mash warm, topped with extra butter.

GARLIC GREEN BEANS

SERVINGS: 6

TIME:
Preparation   10 minutes
Cooking   15 minutes
Total   25 minutes

EQUIPMENT:
Saucepan
Kitchen towel
Sauté pan
Mixing bowl

INGREDIENTS:
1 lb. green beans, trimmed
1 tbsp olive oil
1 shallot, finely chopped
2 clove garlic, finely chopped
1 tbsp unsalted butter
salt, to taste
black pepper, to taste
1 cup ice cubes

INSTRUCTIONS:
1. Fill a saucepan with water, season with salt and place on a high heat.
2. Bring the water to a boil then add the green beans, cook for 2 minutes.
3. Into a mixing bowl add water and top up with ice cubes, transfer the cooked green beans into the iced water to chill.
4. Place a sauté pan on medium heat, add the olive oil and butter.
5. Then add the shallot, cook for 2 minutes to soften.
6. Next add the garlic, cook for 1 minute until fragrant.
7. Toss the green beans into the sauté pan, mix through the shallot and garlic for 2 minutes.
8. Season the garlic green beans with salt and black pepper, serve.

FRIED GREEN TOMATOES

SERVINGS: 8

TIME:
Preparation   20 minutes
Cooking   20 minutes
Total   40 minutes

EQUIPMENT:
Kitchen paper
Mixing bowl x 3
Baking tray
Sauté pan

INGREDIENTS:
5 large green tomatoes, cut into ½-inch slices
1 cup all-purpose flour
2 eggs, lightly beaten
¼ cup milk
¼ cup cornmeal
½ cup breadcrumbs
¼ cup parmesan cheese, grated
½ cup vegetable oil
salt, to taste
black pepper, to taste

INSTRUCTIONS:
1. Place the sliced green tomatoes onto kitchen paper and season with salt.
2. Allow the tomatoes to sit for 10 minutes then pat dry to remove the excess moisture.
3. Prepare three bowls, in the first bowl add the all-purpose flour, salt and black pepper, in the second bowl add the eggs and milk, then in the third bowl add the cornmeal, breadcrumbs, parmesan cheese, salt and black pepper.
4. Dip a slice of green tomato into the flour to cover, shake off the excess.
5. Then dip the floured tomato into the bowl of egg and finally into the bowl of breadcrumbs.
6. Transfer the breaded green tomato onto a tray and repeat from the remaining slices of tomato.
7. Place a sauté pan on medium heat and add the vegetable oil.
8. Lay a few slices of breaded tomato into the sauté pan in a single layer.
9. Cook for 3 minutes until golden brown then flip the green tomatoes and cook for a further 3 minutes.
10. Place the fried green tomatoes on a wire rack to drain, continue to fry the remaining breaded tomato.
11. Serve the fried green tomatoes warm with hot sauce.

GRILLED CORN ON THE COB

SERVINGS: 4

TIME:
Preparation   5 minutes
Cooking   20 minutes
Total   25 minutes

EQUIPMENT:
Grill/Griddle pan
Pastry brush

INGREDIENTS:
1 tsp vegetable oil
4 corn on the cob, shucked and cleaned
¼ cup unsalted butter, melted
salt, to taste

INSTRUCTIONS:
1. Preheat a grill over high heat, move the coals to one side of the grill to create a two-zone cooking space.
2. Whip the grill clean then brush the grates with oil.
3. Place the corn onto the hot side of the grill, char on all sides for 15 minutes.
4. Move the corn to the side of the grill with indirect heat and brush each cob with melted butter.
5. Baste the corn in butter for 5 minutes then season generously with salt.
6. Serve the corn immediately or wrap in aluminum foil to keep warm.

COLLARD GREENS

SERVINGS: 6

TIME:
Preparation   15 minutes
Cooking   1 hour 30 minutes
Total   1 hour 45 minutes

EQUIPMENT:
Saucepan

INGREDIENTS:
2 tbsp olive oil
1 onion, diced
2 cloves garlic, finely chopped
10 oz smoked ham hocks
1 lb. collard green, trimmed and chopped
4 cups chicken broth
1 tbsp apple cider vinegar
salt, to taste
black pepper, to taste

INSTRUCTIONS:
1. Place a saucepan on medium heat and add the olive oil.
2. Then add the onions and cook for 5 minutes to soften.
3. Next add the garlic, cook for 1 minute until fragrant.
4. Stir the smoked ham hock meat to saucepan, season with salt and black pepper, brown for 5 minutes.
5. Into the saucepan add the collard greens and chicken broth.
6. Bring to a simmer and place a lid on the saucepan, cook for 30 minutes.
7. Stir the collard greens and cook uncovered for a further 30 minutes.
8. Once the greens are tender and the broth has reduced, the dish is ready to serve.
9. Shred the smoked ham hocks with a fork then season the collard greens with apple cider vinegar, salt, and black pepper.

BOSTON BEANS

SERVINGS: 12

TIME:
Preparation   20 minutes (overnight to soak)
Cooking   4 hours
Total   4 hours 20 minutes

EQUIPMENT:
Saucepan
Mixing bowl
Casserole dish

INGREDIENTS:
1lb dried navy beans
⅓ cup molasses
¼ cup brown sugar
1 tsp mustard powder
8 oz salt pork, chopped
1 onion, roughly chopped
black pepper, to taste
salt, to taste

INSTRUCTIONS:
1. Place the dried navy beans into a mixing bowl and cover with cold water, soak the beans overnight.
2. The following day, strain the water and rinse the beans.
3. Place the beans into a saucepan and cover with water, set on a medium heat and bring to a boil.
4. Reduce the heat to a light simmer and cook the beans for 30 minutes.
5. Strain the beans and keep the cooking liquid, set both aside.
6. Preheat an oven to 300 degrees Fahrenheit.
7. In a mixing bowl combine the molasses, brown sugar, mustard powder, black pepper, salt and three cups of the bean cooking liquid.
8. Pour the mixture into a casserole dish along with the dried navy beans, salt pork and onion, the beans should be submerged, top up with extra bean cooking liquid if needed.
9. Cover the casserole dish with aluminum foil and place into the preheated oven.
10. Bake the beans on low for 3 hours.
11. Remove the casserole dish from the oven and stir, the beans and pork should be tender, continue to bake and top up with bean cooking liquid until cooked.
12. Serve the baked Boston beans warm.

THREE BEAN SALAD

SERVINGS: 6

TIME:
Preparation   20 minutes
Chill   1 hour
Total   1 hour 20 minutes

EQUIPMENT:
Mixing bowl

INGREDIENTS:
¼ cup red wine vinegar
¼ cup olive oil
½ tsp smoked paprika
1 red onion, thinly sliced
½ cucumber, finely chopped
1 clove garlic, finely chopped
½ cup parsley, finely chopped
14 oz canned cannellini beans, drained and rinsed
14 oz canned kidney beans, drained and rinsed
14 oz canned chickpeas, drained and rinsed
salt, to taste

INSTRUCTIONS:
1. In a mixing bowl stir in the red wine vinegar, olive oil and smoked paprika.
2. Then add the red onion, cucumber, garlic, parsley, cannellini beans, kidney beans and chickpeas.
3. Toss the three-bean salad to combine, season with salt and black pepper.
4. Place the mixing bowl in the refrigerator and allow to chill for at least 1 hour to bring the flavors together.

BAKED ARTICHOKE DIP

SERVINGS: 8

TIME:
Preparation   15 minutes
Cooking   20 minutes
Total   35 minutes

EQUIPMENT:
Baking dish

INGREDIENTS:
1 cup cream cheese, room temperature
1 cup sour cream
¼ cup mayonnaise
2 lb. canned artichoke hearts in water, drained and chopped
1 cup parmesan cheese, grated
1 clove garlic, finely chopped
1 jalapeno, finely chopped
½ cup chives, finely chopped

INSTRUCTIONS:
1. Preheat an oven to 375 degrees Fahrenheit.
2. Into a baking dish add the cream cheese, sour cream, mayonnaise, artichoke hearts, garlic, and jalapeno.
3. Stir the ingredients to combine, then smooth down into an even layer.
4. Place the dish into the preheated oven and bake for 20 minutes.
5. Remove the baked artichoke dip from the oven, garnish with chopped chives then serve as a dip with carrots, celery, toasted bread, or nachos.

THANKSGIVING

When asked as both a chef and firefighter, what is my favorite meal to make, share and enjoy without hesitation, it's Thanksgiving. First, the reason, to give thanks, count one's blessings and be grateful. As a firefighter there certainly are many rewards to this career but it also is fraught with tragedies. As an old Lieutenant once told my brother "We ain't in the business of painting sunsets!" So, on this day, we might put aside our grief, our tragedies and embrace what we have. The other reason Thanksgiving meal...the FOOD! If you love to cook and love to eat, this is your day!

FDNY ENGINE 273/LADDER 129 THANKSGIVING STUFFING

I have had some of my absolute best times and meals in this firehouse and the few Thanksgivings I had to work; it was one of the best places to be on that day. Here is my best stuffing recipe to honor all those I worked with there!

SERVINGS: 8

TIME:
Preparation   15 minutes
Cooking   1 hour 15 minutes
Total   1 hour 30 minutes

EQUIPMENT:
Sauté pan
9"x12" baking dish

INGREDIENTS:
2 tbsp olive oil
½ cup salted butter, softened
1 lb. Italian sausage, removed from casing
2 onions, chopped
7 stalks celery, chopped
4 cloves garlic, minced
6 cups stale French bread, diced into ½-inch cubes
3 cups cornbread, crumbled
1 tbsp dried sage
1 tbsp poultry seasoning
1 cup pine nuts, toasted
4 cups chicken broth
2 cups shredded mozzarella

INSTRUCTIONS:
1. Preheat an oven to 375 degrees Fahrenheit and grease a baking dish with softened butter.
2. Place a sauté pan on medium heat and add the Italian sausage, use a spatula to break up the sausage and brown well for 5 minutes.
3. Transfer the cooked sausage to a bowl and drain away the excess fat.
4. Return the sauté pan to the stove then add the onions, celery, and garlic, cook for 2 minutes to soften.
5. Next add the French bread, cornbread, dried sage, poultry seasoning, pine nuts, cooked sausage, and chicken broth, stir to combine.
6. Pour the stuffing mixture into the greased baking dish and top with shredded mozzarella.
7. Cover the baking dish with aluminum foil and bake for 45 minutes.
8. Remove the foil from the dish and cook for a further 15 minutes until golden brown and bubbling.

ROASTED TURKEY AND GRAVY

Rick Rodgers
Rick is an internationally acclaimed and one of the most versatile professionals in the food business. Through his work as a cooking teacher, food writer, cookbook author (over 40 books), freelance cookbook editor his infectious love of good food reaches countless cooks every day. Rick was of immeasurable help taking a "firehouse" cook like me to a cookbook author! Author of *Thanksgiving 101*, who else would I turn to for the perfect roasted turkey! Visit www. rickrodgers.com.

SERVINGS: 18

TIME:
Preparation   45 minutes
Cooking   4 hours 45 minutes
Total   5 hours 30 minutes

EQUIPMENT:
Wooden skewer
Kitchen string
Aluminum foil
Oven pan and rack

INGREDIENTS:
Turkey
¼ cup unsalted butter, room temperature
8 cups turkey stock
18 lb. turkey
12 cups stuffing

Gravy
¾ cup all-purpose flour
⅓ cup bourbon / port
salt, to taste
black pepper, to taste

INSTRUCTIONS:
Turkey
1. Preheat an oven to 325F, place an oven pan and rack at the base of the oven.
2. Pat the turkey skin dry using kitchen paper then place the turkey breast-side down.
3. Fill the turkey neck cavity with stuffing then pin the neck to the back of the turkey using a wooden skewer to secure.
4. Tuck the turkey wings beside the body and secure with string.
5. Fill the turkey body cavity with stuffing then secure the turkey legs with kitchen string to close the cavity.
6. Rub the turkey skin with softened butter, season with salt and black pepper.
7. Pour two cups of turkey stock into the oven pan then place the turkey on the rack, breast-side up.
8. Cover the turkey with aluminum foil and roast for 30 minutes.
9. Baste the turkey with the roasting juices every 30 minutes, cook for 3 hours.
10. Remove the aluminum foil from the turkey to brown for 1 hour, the turkey is ready when a thermometer reads 180F.
11. Transfer the turkey to a plate and allow it to rest for 20 minutes before serving.

Gravy
1. While the turkey rests, pour the drippings from the roasting pan into a bowl and allow it to settle for 5 minutes.
2. Skim the fat from the surface of the drippings, set aside.
3. Top the drippings with turkey stock to total 8 cups.
4. Place the roasting pan on the stove over a low heat then pour in the skimmed fat.
5. Stir in the flour to deglaze the tray for 2 minutes.
6. Whisk the bourbon, turkey stock and drippings into the roasting pan to form a thick gravy, cook the gravy for 5 minutes.
7. Pour the turkey gravy into a jug and serve alongside the roasted turkey and stuffing.

CAN THE CAN CRANBERRY SAUCE

Please! It's Thanksgiving! This is the easiest way to make fresh cranberry sauce! On this day of gratitude can we "can the cranberry cylinder, store bought cranberry sauce" and make it fresh!

SERVINGS: 6-8

TIME:
Preparation   20 minutes
Cooking   10 minutes
Total   30 minutes

EQUIPMENT:
Saucepan

INGREDIENTS:
12 oz fresh cranberries
½ cup water
½ cup orange juice
½ cup sugar
½ cup brown sugar
1 tsp vanilla extract

INSTRUCTIONS:
1.   Into a saucepan add the cranberries, water, orange juice, sugar, brown sugar, and vanilla extract.
2.   Place the saucepan on medium heat and stir to combine.
3.   Bring the cranberry sauce to a boil then reduce the heat to a simmer, cook for 10 minutes.
4.   Stir to burst the cranberries and thicken, the sauce is ready once it coats the back of a spoon.
5.   Remove the cranberry sauce from the heat and allow it to cool for 20 minutes before serving.

DESSERT

BANANA BREAD PUDDING

SERVINGS: 8

TIME:
Preparation   15 minutes
Cooking   40 minutes
Total   55 minutes

EQUIPMENT:
Mixing bowl
Whisk
Bread tin
Roasting pan

INGREDIENTS:
2 tbsp salted butter, softened
4 eggs
½ cup sugar
2 cups milk
8 oz challah bread, diced into 1-inch cubes
½ fresh vanilla pod, seeds scraped out
2 bananas, thinly sliced
2 cups water, hot

INSTRUCTIONS:
1. Preheat an oven to 350 degrees Fahrenheit and grease a bread tin with butter.
2. In a mixing bowl whisk together the eggs and sugar until thick and creamy.
3. Then gradually pour in the milk, whisk to combine.
4. Next add the cubed challah bread and vanilla seeds, stir, and allow the bread to soak for 5 minutes.
5. After 5 minutes, add the sliced banana to the mixing bowl then transfer the banana bread pudding to the bread tin.
6. Place the bread tin into a shallow roasting pan and fill with hot water to create a water bath, the water should reach halfway up the outside of the bread tin.
7. Transfer the bread pudding to the oven for 40 minutes.
8. Once the banana bread pudding has set, remove from the oven, and allow it to stand for 15 minutes before serving.

FIREHOUSE BREAD PUDDING

This is my best and easiest recipe that I would put against any dessert! Only 8 ingredients! Bread pudding was a "poor man's dessert". During the depression, families would get stale bread from bakers for free and made a dessert from it. You will NOT believe how great stale bread can be!

SERVINGS: 8

TIME:
Preparation   15 minutes
Cooking   1 hour 15 minutes
Total   1 hour 30 minutes

EQUIPMENT:
Saucepan
9"x12" baking dish / cast iron Dutch oven
Mixing bowl
Whisk

INGREDIENTS:
8 oz raisins
3 oz raspberry liqueur (Chambord or Di Amore Raspberry Liqueur)
1 oz unsalted butter, melted
24 oz sliced bread, stale
4 cups heavy cream
3 large eggs
12 oz granulated sugar
1 oz vanilla extract

INSTRUCTIONS:
1. Place a saucepan on low heat then add the raisins and raspberry liqueur, stir to combine.
2. Gradually warm the saucepan to a simmer then remove from the heat, cover with a lid, and set aside.
3. Preheat an oven to 350 degrees Fahrenheit and grease a baking dish with one tablespoon of melted butter.
4. Into a mixing bowl tear the stale sliced bread into bite-sized pieces then add the heavy cream, allow the bread to sit for 5 minutes until soft and absorbed.
5. In a separate bowl whisk together the eggs and sugar until smooth and thick.
6. Then stir in the vanilla extract, remaining melted butter, raisins, and liqueur.
7. Fold in the cream and bread mixture to bring all the ingredients together.
8. Pour the bread pudding into the greased baking dish and place into the oven for 1 hour 15 minutes until browned and set.

RICE PUDDING

SERVINGS: 6

TIME:
Preparation   5 minutes
Cooking   2 hours 30 minutes
Total   2 hours 35 minutes

EQUIPMENT:
Saucepan
Baking dish

INGREDIENTS:
1 tbsp unsalted butter, softened
3 cups milk
½ cup short-grain pudding rice
1 tbsp sugar
1 nutmeg

INSTRUCTIONS:
1. Preheat an oven to 280F and grease a baking dish with butter.
2. Place a saucepan on low heat and add the milk to warm.
3. Into the baking dish add the pudding rice and sugar, then pour the warm milk over the rice and stir to combine.
4. Transfer the baking dish to the oven and bake for 20 minutes.
5. Remove the rice pudding from the oven and stir to separate the grains.
6. Grate fresh nutmeg over the dish then return to the oven for 2 hours.
7. The rice pudding should be well browned and set when ready.

GLAZED DONUT

SERVINGS: 12

TIME:
Preparation   1 hour 30 minutes
Cooking   10 minutes
Total   1 hour 40 minutes

EQUIPMENT:
Jug
Whisk
Mixing bowl
Spatula
Round cutter
Saucepan

INGREDIENTS:
Donut Dough
2 tsp fast action yeast
½ cup water, warm
¼ cup sugar
¼ cup evaporated milk
¼ tsp salt
¼ cup unsalted butter, softened
2 eggs, lightly beaten
½ tsp vanilla extract
2 ½ cups all-purpose flour
4 cups vegetable oil, for frying

Glaze
2 cups icing sugar
⅓ cup milk
½ tsp vanilla extract

INSTRUCTIONS:
1. Preheat an oven to 375 degrees Fahrenheit.
2. In a jug add the yeast, warm water, and sugar, stir to combine then set aside for 10 minutes to activate the yeast.
3. Into a mixing bowl add evaporated milk, salt, butter, eggs, vanilla extract, and all-purpose flour.
4. Pour the yeast mixture into the mixing bowl and use a spatula to bring the dough together.
5. Transfer the dough to a work surface and knead for 5 minutes until smooth and tacky.
6. Return the dough to the mixing bowl and cover with plastic wrap, allow to rest for 1 hour until doubled in size.
7. Turn the dough out onto a work surface and use a rolling pin to roll the dough to ½-inch thick.
8. Use a round cutter to cut the individual donuts from the dough, cover with a kitchen towel and allow to rise for 30 minutes.
9. Fill a saucepan with vegetable oil and place on medium heat, bring the oil to 350 degrees Fahrenheit.
10. In a bowl whisk together the icing sugar, milk, and vanilla extract to form the glaze.
11. Place four donuts into the saucepan of oil, cook in batches for 2 minutes then flip and cook for a further 2 minutes.
12. Remove the fried donut from the saucepan using tongs and place on a wire rack to cool.
13. Whilst still warm, dip the donuts into the glaze then serve.

RED VELVET CAKE

SERVINGS: 8

TIME:
Preparation   1 hour
Cooking   30 minutes
Total   1 hour 30 minutes

EQUIPMENT:
7" cake tin x 2
Mixing bowl x 2
Whisk
Wire cooling rack

INGREDIENTS:
Red Velvet Cake
1 ¼ cups self-rising flour
3 tbsp cocoa powder
1 tsp baking soda
¾ cup sugar
2 eggs
¾ cup vegetable oil
⅔ cup buttermilk
2 tbsp red food coloring

Cream Cheese Frosting
½ cup unsalted butter, softened
4 cups icing sugar
2 cups cream cheese

INSTRUCTIONS:
Red Velvet Cake
1. Preheat an oven to 350 degrees Fahrenheit and line the cake tins with parchment paper.
2. In a mixing bowl add the flour, cocoa powder, baking soda and sugar, stir together.
3. Into a second bowl add the eggs, vegetable oil, buttermilk, and red food coloring, whisk to combine.
4. Stir the bowl of wet ingredients into the bowl of dry, beat together to form a smooth batter.
5. Transfer the cake batter evenly into the two cake tins then place in the preheated oven for 30 minutes.
6. Remove the cakes from the oven and cool on a wire rack.

Cream Cheese Frosting
1. In a bowl whisk together the softened butter and icing sugar until thick and smooth.
2. Then stir the cream cheese into the frosting to combine.
3. Once the cakes have cooled, spread a layer of cream cheese on the base of one cake and place the second on top.
4. Cover the cake in cream frosting and chill in the refrigerator before serving.

BANANA FOSTER

SERVINGS: 4

TIME:
Preparation   5 minutes
Cooking   10 minutes
Total   15 minutes

EQUIPMENT:
Sauté pan

INGREDIENTS:
¼ cup unsalted butter
¼ cup brown sugar
4 bananas, sliced
3 oz dark rum
4 cups vanilla ice cream
¼ tsp ground cinnamon

INSTRUCTIONS:
1. Place a sauté pan on medium heat then add the butter and brown sugar.
2. Stir the mixture and melt the butter to form a light caramel.
3. Lay the bananas into the sauté pan, cook for 1 minute.
4. Flip the bananas and caramelize the other side for 30 seconds.
5. Remove the pan from the heat and pour in the dark rum.
6. Return the sauté pan to the heat, reduce the rum by half.
7. Serve the banana foster over a scoop of vanilla ice cream then dust over ground cinnamon.

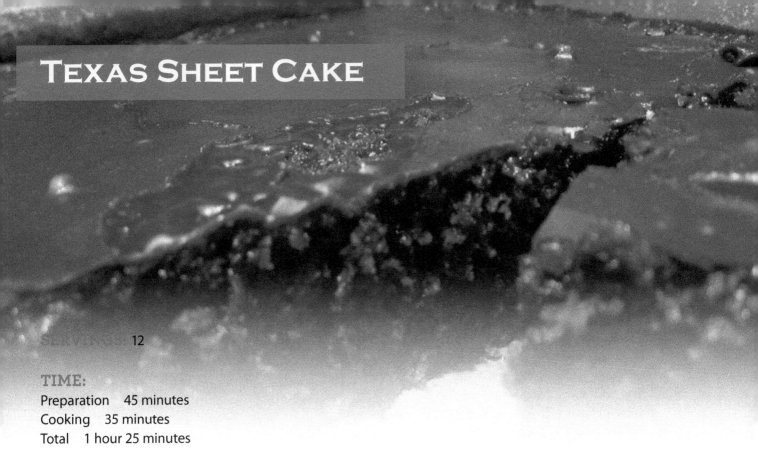

TEXAS SHEET CAKE

TIME:
Preparation   45 minutes
Cooking   35 minutes
Total   1 hour 25 minutes

EQUIPMENT:
Mixing bowl x 2
13"x18" sheet pan
Whisk
Spatula
Wire cooling rack

INGREDIENTS:

Texas Sheet Cake
1 tsp vanilla extract
2 cups all-purpose flour
2 cups sugar
½ cup cocoa powder
2 tsp baking soda
½ tsp salt
1 cup unsalted butter, melted
1 cup buttermilk
½ cup sour cream
2 eggs

Chocolate Frosting
¼ cup milk
½ cup unsalted butter
¼ cup cocoa powder
½ tsp vanilla extract
4 cups icing sugar
1 cup pecans

INSTRUCTIONS:

1. Preheat an oven to 350 degrees Fahrenheit and grease a sheet tray with one tablespoon of softened butter.
2. In a mixing bowl add the flour, sugar, cocoa powder, baking soda and salt, stir to combine.
3. In a set mixing bowl whisk together the melted butter, buttermilk, sour cream, eggs, and vanilla extract.
4. Pour the bowl of wet ingredients into the bowl of dry ingredients, whisk together into a smooth batter.
5. Bake the Texas sheet cake for 20 minutes in the preheated oven.
6. Remove the cake from the oven and allow it to cool on a wire rack.
7. Place a saucepan on low heat then add the milk and butter.
8. Once the butter has melted, remove the saucepan from the stove and stir in the cocoa powder and vanilla extract.
9. Gradually add the icing sugar into the saucepan, whisking to form a thick frosting.
10. While the sheet cake is still warm, spread the chocolate frosting over the surface of the cake.
11. Scatter pecans over the Texas sheet cake then cool at room temperature for 30 minutes to set.

POSA Cheesecake

Probationary Firefighters Kenny Gianelli, Thomas Pellegrino and Joseph Bonanno at Randalls Island Fire Academy. Nicknamed the "Italian Battalion"

Thomas Pellegrino FDNY Engine 290/Ladder 103 POSA... Pride of Sheffield Avenue, Brooklyn, one of NYC busiest firehouses. Tom was assigned there from Probie School. We had become friends while training for the test and he was one of my best motivators to become a firefighter, for which I thank him to this day!

SERVINGS: 12

TIME:
Preparation   30 minutes
Cooking   1 hour
Total   1 hour 30 minutes

EQUIPMENT:
Saucepan
Spring-form tin
Mixing bowl x 2
Spatula

INGREDIENTS:
Crust
¼ cup unsalted butter, softened
1 cup graham crackers, crushed

Cheesecake
⅔ cup heavy cream
1 lb. cream cheese, softened
½ cup sugar
2 eggs
1 tsp vanilla extract

INSTRUCTIONS:
Crust
1. Grease a spring-form tin with one tablespoon of softened butter.
2. Then add the butter to a saucepan and place on a low heat until melted.
3. Stir the crushed graham cracker into the melted butter then transfer to the base of the spring-form tin.
4. Spread the biscuit crust across the base and press firmly into an even layer.

Cheesecake
1. Preheat an oven to 325F.
2. In a mixing bowl add the heavy cream, whisk to lightly whip then set aside.
3. Into a second mixing bowl add the cream cheese, mix with a spatula to soften then add the sugar.
4. Beat the sugar into the cream cheese to dissolve then add the vanilla extract and eggs, beat for 1 minute.
5. Pour the whipped cream into the bowl of cheese mixture and fold together.
6. Transfer the cheese mixture into the spring-form tin and smooth down with a spatula.
7. Bake the New York cheesecake in the preheated oven for 1 hour.
8. Remove the cheesecake from the oven and allow to cool at room temperature, then place in the oven to chill.
9. Release the cheesecake from the spring-form tin, slice and serve.

CHOCOLATE SPONGE CAKE

SERVINGS: 8

TIME:
Preparation   30 minutes
Cooking   30 minutes
Total   1 hour

EQUIPMENT:
7" cake tin x 2
Mixing bowl
Whisk
Wire cooling rack
Saucepan

INGREDIENTS:
Chocolate Sponge Cake
½ cup cocoa powder
½ cup water, hot
3 eggs
1 ½ cups sugar
⅓ cup unsalted butter, softened
2 tbsp milk
1 tsp baking powder
1 ½ cups self-rising flour

Chocolate Frosting
⅔ cup heavy cream
1 cup chocolate, broken into pieces

INSTRUCTIONS:
Chocolate Sponge Cake
1. Preheat an oven to 350 degrees Fahrenheit and grease the cake tin with softened butter.
2. In a mixing bowl add the cocoa powder and hot water, stir to dissolve the chocolate into a thick paste.
3. Then add the eggs, sugar, softened butter, milk, baking powder and flour.
4. Beat the mixture with a whisk until thick and smooth.
5. Transfer the cake batter into the two cake tins, spread out into an even layer.
6. Bake the cakes for 30 minutes.
7. Remove the cakes from the oven and cool on a wire rack.

Chocolate Frosting
1. Pour the heavy cream into a saucepan and place on a medium heat.
2. Warm the cream then remove the saucepan from the heat and add the chocolate.
3. Stir to melt the chocolate into a thick ganache.
4. Spread half of the chocolate frosting over one of the cakes then place the second cake on top of the first.
5. Then cover the cake in chocolate frosting and refrigerate before serving.

PEACH COBBLER

SERVINGS: 6

TIME:
Preparation   15 minutes
Cooking   20 minutes
Total   35 minutes

EQUIPMENT:
Mixing bowl
Cast iron skillet
Whisk

INGREDIENTS:

Peaches
5 large peaches, halved and pitted
1 tbsp orange zest
½ tsp ground cinnamon
½ cup caster sugar

Cobbler
½ cup unsalted butter
½ cup plain flour
1 cup milk
½ cup brown sugar
2 tsp baking powder
1 tsp ground cinnamon
½ tsp salt

INSTRUCTIONS:

1. In a bowl combine the peaches, orange zest, ½ tsp ground cinnamon and caster sugar.
2. Preheat an oven to 400 degrees Fahrenheit and place a skillet on the stove at medium heat.
3. Place the butter in the skillet and warm through until melted.
4. Then add the sugared peaches to the skillet, cook for 5 minutes to form a syrup.
5. In a mixing bowl add the milk, brown sugar, plain flour, baking powder, cinnamon, and salt. Whisk together the ingredients to form a thick, smooth batter then pour the batter.
6. Pour the batter into the skillet to cover the peaches.
7. Transfer the peach cobbler to the preheated oven and bake for 15 minutes until a golden crust has formed.
8. Remove the peach cobbler from the oven and allow to stand for 10 minutes, serve warm with custard or vanilla ice cream.

CHOCOLATE CHIP COOKIES

SERVINGS: 16

TIME:
Preparation   20 minutes
Cooking   10 minutes
Total   30 minutes

EQUIPMENT:
Mixing bowl
Spatula
Whisk
Sieve
Baking tray x 2

INGREDIENTS:
⅔ cup unsalted butter, softened
⅓ cup brown sugar
⅓ cup sugar
2 tsp vanilla extract
1 egg
1 ½ cups all-purpose flour
½ tsp baking soda
¼ tsp salt
1 cup chocolate chips

INSTRUCTIONS:
1. Preheat an oven to 375 degrees Fahrenheit and line two baking trays with parchment paper.
2. Into a bowl add the butter, brown sugar, and sugar, stir together using a spatula in smooth and creamy.
3. Then add the vanilla extract and egg, mix to combine.
4. Into a sieve add the all-purpose flour, baking soda and salt, dust into the mixing bowl then stir together to form a smooth dough.
5. Fold the chocolate chips into the dough.
6. Spoon one tablespoon of the dough onto the baking sheet and repeat for all the mixture, separating each cookie by 2 inches to allow for spreading.
7. Transfer the baking trays to the oven and bake for 10 minutes.
8. Remove the chocolate chip cookies from the oven and allow them to cool for 15 minutes before serving.

Apple Pie

SERVINGS: 8

TIME:
Preparation   1 hour 30 minutes
Cooking   1 hour 30 minutes
Total   3 hours

EQUIPMENT:
Mixing bowl
8"x8" Pie dish
Wire cooling rack
Rolling pin
Pastry brush

INGREDIENTS:
1 lb. apples, peeled and sliced ¼-inch thick
⅓ cup brown sugar
1 tsp ground cinnamon
½ tsp salt
1 tbsp cornstarch
1 tbsp unsalted butter, softened
18 oz pie crust dough
1 tbsp all-purpose flour, for dusting
1 egg, lightly beaten

INSTRUCTIONS:
1. Into a mixing bowl add the apples, brown sugar, cinnamon, and salt, toss to coat the apples then set aside for 30 minutes.
2. Split the pie crust dough in half, place half on a work surface and dust with flour, roll out to ½-inch thick.
3. Grease a pie dish with softened butter then lay the dough into the pie dish, use the sides of your fingers to press the dough into the dish then trim the edges.
4. Cover the pie dish with plastic wrap and place in the refrigerator for 30 minutes.
5. Preheat an oven to 400 degrees Fahrenheit.
6. Remove the chilled pie crust from the refrigerator and line with parchment paper then fill with baking beans.
7. Place the pie dish in the preheated oven and bake for 15 minutes.
8. Then remove the baking beans from the pie dish and bake from a further 15 minutes until lightly golden.
9. Allow the pie dish to cool on a wire rack.
10. Once the pastry has cooled, stir the cornstarch into the bowl of apples to thicken the sauce then pour the apples into the pie base.
11. Roll the second half of the pie crust dough to 1-inch thick then lay over the top of the pie dish.
12. Use a fork to seal the edges and pierce a hole in the center of the pastry.
13. Brush the pastry with a lightly beaten egg then place in the oven.
14. Bake the apple pie for 1 hour until the pastry is crisp and the apples are tender.
15. Allow the apple pie to cool before serving.

BLUE RIBBON CARROT CAKE

SERVINGS: 8

TIME:
Preparation   30 minutes
Cooking   30 minutes
Total   1 hour

EQUIPMENT:
Mixing bowl x 2
Cake tin x 3

INGREDIENTS:

Carrot Cake
2 cups brown sugar
1 cup vegetable oil
4 eggs, lightly beaten
½ cup applesauce
2 cups plain flour
2 tsp baking powder
2 tsp baking soda
1 tsp salt
1 tsp ground cinnamon
1 tsp ground nutmeg
1 tsp ground ginger
1 tsp vanilla extract
3 cups grated carrot

Cream Cheese Frosting
1lb cream cheese, room temperature
½ cup unsalted butter, room temperature
1 tsp vanilla extract
4 cups icing sugar
2 cups pecans, roughly chopped

I entered this cake in the very first FDNY Bake Off in 1994 and won a first place Blue Ribbon. One of the judges was the late John Sineno Engine 58 FDNY, who was the first firefighter to achieve national recognition for cooking with his book *The Firefighters Cookbook* in 1986.

INSTRUCTIONS:
1. Preheat an oven to 350 degrees Fahrenheit and grease three cake tins.
2. In a mixing bowl whisk together the brown sugar, vegetable oil, applesauce, and eggs.
3. In a separate bowl combine the plain flour, baking powder, baking soda, salt, cinnamon, nutmeg, and ginger.
4. Fold together the wet and dry ingredients to form a smooth batter.
5. Stir the vanilla extract and grated carrot into the cake batter then pour evenly between the three cake tins.
6. Bake the carrot cakes for 30 minutes in the preheated oven.
7. Remove the cakes from the oven and allow to cool on a wire rack.
8. While the carrot cake cools, prepare the cream cheese frosting. In a mixing bowl whisk together the cream cheese, butter, and vanilla extract until smooth.
9. Then pour the icing sugar into the cream cheese, fold together to create a thick smooth frosting.
10. Onto one of the cakes spread a thick layer of cream cheese frosting, then position a second cake on top of the first to stack them together.
11. Spread a second layer of cream cheese frosting over the top of the second cake then add the final cake as a third tier.
12. Once the cakes are stacked, spread the remaining cream cheese frosting to cover the whole cake.
13. Using your hands, press the chopped pecans into the sides of the carrot cake and refrigerate for 20 minutes before serving.

NORMANGO COBBLER

SERVINGS: 6

TIME:
Preparation   20 minutes
Cooking   25 minutes
Total   45 minutes

EQUIPMENT:
Mixing bowl
9" baking dish

INGREDIENTS:
4 large ripe mangos, peeled and sliced
1 tsp ground ginger
1 ½ tsp ground cinnamon
½ cup orange juice, freshly squeezed
1 cup all-purpose flour
1 tbsp sugar
½ tsp pink salt
1 ½ tsp baking powder
3 tbsp unsalted butter, room temperature
½ cup half and half milk
¼ cup confectioner's sugar

Why Mangoes? As a fitness trainer and nutritionist, certainly the many health benefits, full of Vitamin C and great for digestion. Having relocated to Florida, I planted a small mango tree, not more than a foot high in my yard, that I had gotten at a flea market. It's grown quite large and produces the most delicious mangoes I have ever eaten. Great on their own but I came up with a great way to have them for dessert!

INSTRUCTIONS:
1. Preheat an oven to 350 degrees Fahrenheit and grease a baking dish with softened butter.
2. Into the baking dish add the mango, ginger, cinnamon, and orange juice, toss together to coat.
3. In a mixing bowl stir the flour, sugar, salt, and baking powder.
4. Crumble the softened butter into the flour, use the tips of your fingers to bring the mixture together into a "sandy" texture.
5. Mix the milk into the bowl of flour until smooth.
6. Use a spoon to cover the mango with the dough mixture, spread out over the top.
7. Place the baking dish into the preheated oven for 25 minutes until golden brown.
8. Remove the mango cobbler from the oven and dust with confectioner's sugar, serve warm.

ZUCCHINI BREAD

SERVINGS: 2 loaves

TIME:
Preparation   20 minutes
Cooking   1 hour
Total   1 hour 20 minutes

EQUIPMENT:
Mixing bowl x 2
Loaf tin x 2
Spatula
Wire cooling rack

INGREDIENTS:
3 large eggs
2 cups zucchini, peeled and grated
2 cups sugar
2 tsp vanilla extract
1 cup vegetable oil
3 cups all-purpose flour
2 tsp ground cinnamon
1 tsp baking powder
1 tsp baking soda
½ tsp salt

Harbor Dish in a community food bank/service in Safety Harbor, FL. I am a volunteer there and have tremendous assistance from the many other volunteers. One of them, Lara, makes an outstanding and easy to make Zucchini Bread. Visit the website at www.harbordish.org.

INSTRUCTIONS:
1. Preheat an oven to 325 and grease two loaf tins with softened butter.
2. In a mixing bowl add the eggs, beat until light and fluffy.
3. Then add the zucchini, sugar, vanilla extract, and vegetable oil, fold the ingredients together to combine.
4. In a separate mixing bowl stir in the flour, ground cinnamon, baking powder, baking soda and salt.
5. Pour the flour mixture into the bowl of zucchini, mix using a spatula to form a batter.
6. Transfer the zucchini bread batter into the two loaf tins then place in the preheated oven.
7. Bake the zucchini bread for 1 hour then remove from the oven.
8. Rest the zucchini bread on a wire cooling rack and allow it to cool before serving.

In Memoriam
Michael Bonanno Ladder 7
Fire Department City of New York